Primary Health Care

Reorienting organisational support

Edited by
G.J. Ebrahim
J.P. Ranken

MACMILLAN
PUBLISHERS

First published 1988

Published by *Macmillan Publishers Ltd*
London and Basingstoke
*Associated companies and representatives in Accra,
Auckland, Delhi, Dublin, Gaborone, Hamburg, Harare,
Hong Kong, Kuala Lumpur, Lagos, Manzini, Melbourne,
Mexico City, Nairobi, New York, Singapore, Tokyo*

Printed in Hong Kong

British Library Cataloguing in Publication Data
Primary health care: reorienting organisational
  support.
  1. Health services administration —
  Developing countries
  I. Ebrahim, G.J.   II. Ranken, J.P.
  362.1'09172'4   RA395.D44

ISBN 0-333-46210-6

Acknowledgements

Fig. 5.1 is from *Social and Community Paediatrics* by G.J. Ebrahim
(Macmillan Education) 1985.
All the remaining figures were prepared by the Tropical Child Health Unit,
Institute of Child Health, University of London and are used with
permission.
The authors and publishers would like to thank CAFOD for a generous
subsidy allowing this to be published as a low cost book.

Dedicated to
The World Health Organisation
on its
40th anniversary.

Contributors

JUSTUS AKINSANYA is currently Principal Lecturer in Nursing and Director of Studies at the Institute of Higher Education in Poole, Dorset. He is the author of two nursing textbooks published by Macmillan.

ANNE BAMISAIYE is a social scientist who has worked in Nigeria in medical education and health care delivery since 1968. She is an Associate Professor within the Institute of Child Health and Primary Care, College of Medicine, University of Lagos where she is a member of the team organising and teaching a six month programme in Primary Health Care for Final Year medical undergraduates.

BRIAN DONALD is a manager/administrator with experience in health services and education as a practitioner, consultant, university teacher and researcher. From September 1986 he has been a Senior Research Fellow in the Centre for Health Planning and Management, University of Keele.

G.J. EBRAHIM is currently Reader at the Institute of Child Health, London and also joint editor of the Journal of Tropical Paediatrics. At the Institute he is responsible for the course in Mother and Child Health leading to the MSc degree at the University of London. He was involved in establishing the Child Health Services in Tanzania at Independence as well as the Department of Paediatrics at the Dar es Salaam School of Medicine. He is the author of a number of paediatrics textbooks published by Macmillan.

MARIE-THÉRÈSE FEUERSTEIN has been a regular consultant to WHO, FAO and international voluntary agencies in international health, primary health care, participatory evaluation, adult education etc. She has experience in many parts of the world particularly in SE Asia and Central America. She is the author of *Partners in Evaluation*, published by Macmillan.

GOURI GUPTA has extensive teaching experience at postgraduate level in India and abroad. He has a wide range of publications in the area of

iv

management. Besides teaching, his major interests are training, consultancy and research in the area of health services management.

ROBIN GOURLAY is Professor of Health Care Management at the International Management Centre, Buckingham.

TONY KLOUDA is a medical doctor. He spent five years in Tanzania as an Oxfam Medical Adviser, working with governmental and non-governmental agencies as well as villagers on approaches to health. He then spent four years in Malawi as PHC coordinator for the Private Hospitals Association of Malawi. In this capacity he also joined in on developing and implementing a national approach to PHC for Malawi. He is currently Coordinator of the AIDS unit at the International Planned Parenthood Federation, London.

BARNEY McCAUGHEY helped initially with the location and development of new industry in Ireland and has worked in the Health and Social Services. He then joined the Industrial Training Service of which he is now the Director. He has extensive experience including a large voluntary element of working with community and voluntary organisations and helping them take ownership of managing their own health and development.

JOHN RANKEN is Senior Lecturer in Management at the Institute of Child Health, London, having had previous experience in personnel and management training in the UK National Health Service (1971–82) and Zambia (1968–70). He recently completed a three year research project on The Work and Support of District Health Managers in Kenya, Bombay and Zambia.

FRED ROACH is Course Tutor, Advanced Nursing Administration and Health Service Administration at the Institute of Advanced Nursing Education, Royal College of Nursing of the United Kingdom.

Contents

Formal and non-formal education sectors; Adult education and community involvement; Community development and women's development; Housing; Water, sanitation and environment; Information and media; Industry and commerce; Non-governmental and private sector; Building on experience

Chapter 10 NGOs and International Organisations 146

Initiating and supporting change; NGOs as representatives; The impact of PHC on NGOs; The contribution of NGOs to country health programmes; The impact of NGOs internationally

Chapter 11 Challenges for the Future 158

Avoiding the pitfalls; The management of change; Entering the 1990s; New issues to be addressed

Preface

A great deal has been written about Primary Health Care since the Alma-Ata Declaration in 1978. All the nations of the world were represented at the meeting and discussions ranged far and wide. The unanimity of the decision indicates that Primary Health Care is considered desirable and possible in all types of political, social, economic and cultural environments. A number of publications by the World Health Organisation in the series 'Health for All' provide clarification on strategies, managerial processes, monitoring and evaluation. There has also been a wealth of literature in scientific journals and in the form of books. This is because the concept of Primary Health Care did not appear out of the blue. It represents a large number of innovative developments and the distillation of experiences from around the world. Primary Health Care is more than a programme. It entails change. It requires changes in concepts and ways of thinking. Its implementation is a process which calls for wide ranging changes in established systems and institutions as well as in communities.

There is no single blueprint for Primary Health Care. Countries are usually able to establish Primary Health Care when there is enough national commitment and first hand experience. Often the latter is through projects which together become a 'critical mass'. In some countries academic institutions have led the way. In others national solidarity and political cohesion provided a springboard for Primary Health Care. In several countries non-governmental organisations have played a crucial role.

It has been necessary to record experiences and identify the positive as well as negative influences in the implementation of Primary Health Care. Out of such an analysis the more significant pathways may be identified. The Tropical Child Health Unit of the Institute of Child Health in London has a long record of providing teaching material for the developing world. Our own training programme in Mother and Child Health carries a strong component on Primary Health Care. Several members of the Unit are involved with a number of national authorities in organising Primary Health Care programmes which have provided a rich experience. These and other involvements led to the seed of the idea for a book on Primary Health Care with an emphasis on how countries can reorient their health services towards this ideal. A group of contributors was identified and invited to address this issue. The contributors were asked to write on a topic according to their interest and experience. All the contributions were received in time demonstrating the keenness and devotion of the contributors to their subject. The text was then enlarged upon and rewritten followed by editing to form a cohesive whole. The final responsibility for what is said in the book must therefore rest with the two of us.

The contributors commented on the final text as well as on the chapters in which their own contributions were included. As such this is a joint effort. The contributions to chapters were as follows:

B. McCaughey and R. Gourlay − Theory and Practice of Organisational Change

G. Gupta − Ministries of Health and Primary Health Care

B. Donald − Hospitals and Primary Health Care

A. Bamisaiye − Medical Education for Primary Health Care

F. Roach and J. Akinsanya − Nursing Models for Primary Health Care

M.-T. Feuerstein − Intersectoral Collaboration

A. Klouda − Non-Governmental and International Organisations

We acknowledge our debt to the contributors who together constituted the Study Group in Management of Change for PHC.

The book should appeal to a wide range of readers, commencing from those involved in day-to-day running of community health activities to officials in decision making positions in Ministries of Health and non-governmental organisations; from those involved in management of health programmes to leaders in institutions of medical training. It should also appeal to aid agencies and international organisations who are confronted with the difficult task of helping to bring about appropriate change.

G.J.E./J.P.R.

CHAPTER 1
Introduction

Ten years have passed since Primary Health Care (PHC) was first defined at the Alma-Ata Conference. Since then a number of countries have evolved strategies and plans for establishing primary health care with varying levels of success. In 1985 the World Health Organisation (WHO) completed a 'Review of PHC'. Out of 166 member states of WHO 146 participated in the exercise and a great deal of progress has been reported. Such evaluations have shown that many of the problems of PHC are concerned with the management of PHC and with the reorientation of already established services to PHC. An analysis of some of the management problems shows that they are deep seated and require a fundamental reappraisal of the existing systems.

WHO's call for 'Health for All by the year 2000' heralds the greatest exercise in management by objectives undertaken on a global scale. Many countries have responded with national policies, statements of intent and plans for including PHC into the national planning process. But there has often been less success in the translation of these plans into actions, except in the case of a few countries and several pilot projects. Whereas the pilot projects have helped to evolve the basic technology of PHC and have provided a measure of the required administrative support, there has been less evidence of success in applying the lessons learned throughout a whole health system.

Central to the concept of PHC is that individuals, families and communities take the major responsibility for their own health. The role of the health professionals, and health systems is to assist and support this process. The implications of this concept are serious for a health system which has monopolised health care. New roles are now being demanded of health professionals and institutions. Their functions must change from being providers to enablers. Enabling skills and methods are not widely understood and taught within the present health systems.

Methods and techniques of working with communities have much in common with those of working in large organisations, even though the way in which they are applied would vary greatly from place to place. PHC asks for a bottom-up approach for setting targets and identifying needs. They in turn determine top-down actions and decisions. In other words health systems and related organisations need to set their objectives and determine their activities in relation to those expressed by the communities which they serve. Such a working style calls for a continuing process of dialogue, popular consultation, organisational adaptation and change.

PHC must not be confused with first contact care. Eight specific elements of PHC were identified at Alma-Ata. At the level of the individual, the family and the community these eight elements must come together to constitute PHC. At the level of the central bureaucracy each element may exist in a separate government ministry. Hence intersectoral collaboration is a key element of PHC. Because of rigid compartmentalism in government ministries there has been more discussion than action with regard to collaboration between sectors. A great deal of health improvement requires actions outside the health sector. Hence flexibility and adaptation in long established bureaucracies are essential. For an uninhibited development of PHC it may be necessary to take a careful look at existing organisations and structures, both within the administration and at the community level.

The arguments advanced in this book would stress that the health sector has a clear responsibility of putting its house in order in relation to PHC, and then to work through in detail the implications of its PHC policy. Within the health system there is evidence of much vitality in certain places and inertia in others. The former can become growth points for change in the future. The roles of hospitals, training institutions and the ministries of health need to be clearly defined and methods of developing management skills at each level should be identified.

Change is not easy. Fortunately there is much experience to go by in the way change has been brought about in many systems and organisations around the world. Accelerating change is one of the features of industrial societies, and techniques of dealing with change have been evolved in some detail in many large organisations. Much of this experience may not be directly transferable but a number of principles and concepts may have relevance for the Third World. Already several countries have adopted the health programming approach as a way of adapting this technology of change and the same has been happening with regard to programmes of community development.

At the practical level action programmes for reorienting health systems towards PHC must commence at the smallest manageable unit. In most countries this unit is the district. It is within the district that the initiatives of the central planning units face the realities of implementation; where policies are being converted into action, and where the interface with the community is not too far away. In many ways the district is also a self-contained segment of the national health system. Several countries are now concentrating their efforts on building up the district health infrastructure in keeping with the requirements of PHC. Decentralisation for generating district level

2

initiative is linking up with community participation to respond to local needs, instead of empirical targets. However, the district level administration is also the weakest segment with regard to planning and managerial skills. In order to respond effectively to the need for change countries are using a variety of methods to provide these skills at the district level.

Documentation of the process of organisational change in health services is at a relatively early stage. This book does not set out to prescribe what should be done. Rather it sets out to provide descriptions of a number of projects where change has been successfully accomplished, and will attempt to draw principles from them. The book often will describe the current 'state of the art' with regard to reorientation methods which have been successful.

CHAPTER 2
Primary Health Care and Change

'Primary Health Care is essential health care based on practical, scientifically sound and socially acceptable methods and technology, made universally accessible to individuals and families in the community through their full participation and at a cost that the community and country can afford to maintain at every stage of their development in the spirit of self-reliance and self-determination.'

WHO-UNICEF, 1978

The sequence of events and developments leading to the evolution of the concept of Primary Health Care is well known. At the time of independence many pre-colonial countries in the Third World had inherited a health system largely intended for the colonial administrators, the military and the civilian elite. The large bulk of the population had to make do with whatever rudimentary form of health care was available largely in the private sector, the traditional systems and home remedies. The concept of the Health Centre had evolved in the fifties and in some countries early developments in preventive/promotive medicine had taken place. At independence the national leadership in all countries had made a commitment to better health for the people. Consequently, early developments in the health infrastructure took place along two main paths viz. (a) along conventional lines − the growth of hospitals was associated with improvements in the quality of care and the development of centres of excellence, for example in India, Indonesia, and most of south-east Asia, (b) the building of health centres and their satellite centres including health posts as in Tanzania, Zambia, and many countries of sub-Saharan Africa.

Unplanned creation of health infrastructure together with the trends in administration inherited from the past soon led to several disparities.

Firstly, there arose the disparity between expenditure and needs. In most countries more than three-quarters of the health budget was being spent on hospitals which were mainly urban and catered for disease whereas the need was for prevention, improved nutrition, personal hygiene and environmental sanitation. Preventive services like the under-fives' clinics and antenatal care did not receive much emphasis in the national health plans.

Secondly, there was the disparity between resource allocation and population distribution. Most of the health personnel and capital resources remained sequestered in the urban areas catering for the elite even though the population was largely rural, or lived in urban squatter areas. A large share of the annual recurrent expenditure went into servicing the capital resources.

The third disparity arose on account of rapid population growth and the accompanying slow growth of services. Because of the hospital oriented and hence capital intensive model of health infrastructure which was adopted, the growth in services was of necessity slow. Moreover, health planners came under pressure because of the overcrowding of hospital services and lacked the necessary epidemiological insights to notice the worsening state of services in peri-urban and rural areas.

Because of these and many other disparities a different approach to provision of health care was looked for, and towards the late sixties the concept of Basic Health Services (BHS) evolved. Adequate coverage with simple preventive/promotive services like under-fives' clinics, antenatal care, immunisation, care during labour and so on were the main objectives of BHS. Such care did not require highly skilled personnel nor expensive technology. Already several countries near to the eastern seaboard of Africa, for example Sudan, Somalia, Uganda, Kenya, Tanzania, Malawi, Zambia, Lesotho as well as others like Papua New Guinea were demonstrating that the medical auxiliary could be the back-bone of a national health service. But the services continued to remain largely institutionalised, and in many countries the health centres and sub-centres ended up by providing mainly ambulatory curative care.

In the early seventies experiences in other sectors and insight into the development process had profound influence on the health sector. Firstly, the 'strategy of modernisation' and its corollary the 'trickle down process' were shown to be not working. In country after country the dream of 'economic miracle' was turning into the nightmare of 'permanent debt' and dependency. Clearly an alternative approach to development was needed. Secondly, countries like China and Cuba were demonstrating that a turn-around in health and improvement in the quality of life of the average citizen was possible. In 1975 a joint WHO-UNICEF study had estimated that only about a fifth of the rural populations in developing countries received any basic health care on a regular basis. The study then went on to describe case studies of alternative approaches to health development in ten countries and drew several important conclusions from them. This was followed in 1976 by a study from the International Labour Organisation (ILO) which estimated that almost two-thirds of the populations of the developing countries were living in serious poverty and 700 million of them were destitutes with incomes more than 50 per cent below the poverty line. The multiple deprivations suffered by such families were identified and their stunting effects on the potential for growth and development were described. Based on the study the ILO advocated a 'Basic Needs' approach to national development.

The convergence of new thinking in human development and alternative strategies in health planning together with several countries' experiences evolved into the Primary Health Care approach set out in the Alma-Ata

ADEQUATE
WATER SUPPLY

ADEQUATE
NUTRITION

SAFE
SANITATION

IMMUNISATION
AGAINST MAJOR
DISEASES

MATERNAL AND
CHILD CARE AND
FAMILY PLANNING
ADVICE

COMMUNITY PARTICIPATION
IN DECIDING ON AND
SUPPORTING PREVENTATIVE
HEALTH PLANS

BACK-UP REFERRAL
SERVICE FOR TRAINING
OF PRIMARY HEALTH
CARE WORKERS AND FOR
HEALTH PROBLEMS
REQUIRING MORE
QUALIFIED CARE

TREATMENT FOR
CUTS AND
COMMON AILMENTS

PARENTAL EDUCATION
IN NUTRITION AND
PREVENTATIVE HEALTH
METHODS

Fig. 2.1   Elements of PHC

6

conference in 1978. PHC was to '.... address the main health problems in the community providing promotive, preventive, curative and rehabilitative services'. Eight activities (Fig. 2.1) were identified as the main focus of PHC as follows:

1. Promotion of nutrition.
2. Provision of adequate supply of safe water.
3. Provision of basic sanitation.
4. Maternal and child care including family planning.
5. Immunisation against the major infectious diseases.
6. Prevention and control of locally endemic diseases.
7. Education concerning the prevalent health problems and the methods of their prevention and control.
8. Appropriate treatment for common diseases and injuries.

   PHC as defined above embodies the basic needs approach and the provision of essential health services with community involvement and participation. Whereas the BHS approach of the sixties was a development away from hospitals towards health centres and sub-centres using auxiliary personnel, PHC is a drive towards the front-line of day-to-day activities carried out within the community.

The three areas of activities in PHC

Taken together the eight elements of PHC fall into three main interacting areas of activity viz.:

1. Co-ordination and collaboration with other sectors for example agriculture, water and sanitation, community development, roads and transport, education and so on.
2. Establishing firm roots within the community with active involvement and participation of the people to encourage self-reliance.
3. Wholehearted support from the formal health system with regard to training, logistics and referral of problems.

Future framework for health services

The PHC approach goes further than the mere amalgamation of the Basic Needs approach with the concept of Basic Health Services. It identifies the main framework for health services as follows:

1. The gross inequality in the health status of people within countries and between countries cannot be accepted. There is an urgent need for improving the health and welfare of the rural and urban poor, and of communities living in remote areas by universal accessibility of services embodying the eight elements of PHC. Hence the issues of equity, availability of services and their acceptability need to be addressed.
2. In the process of making health care more widely available for the purpose of equity, the mass of the people should be the major activists

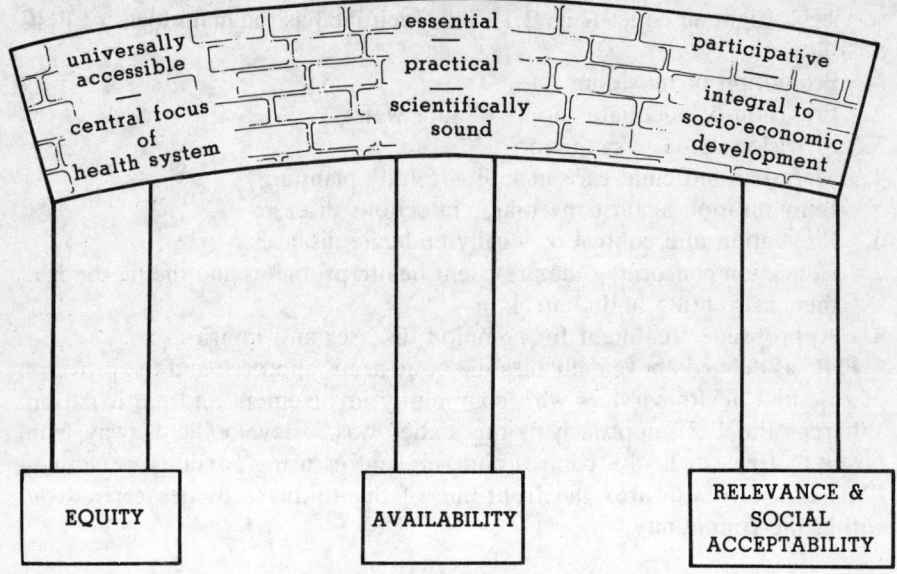

Fig. 2.2   Framework of health services in PHC

as well as the main beneficiaries. Health is not to be 'delivered' to people by health professionals and their assistants, but the people have a right to participate individually and collectively, for example women, men, youth, etc. in shaping their future health.

3.   The promotion of health depends also on improving the socio-economic conditions and therefore a co-ordinated effort is needed from other social and economic sectors.

4.   Such a co-ordinated effort by several governmental departments requires the political commitment of the State as a whole, and hence the need for the creation of a national will (Fig. 2.2).

The political challenge of PHC

A great deal of determination and a total reorientation of approach in policy formulation are needed for the management of PHC related activities and the mobilisation of communities. Countries which have thought that PHC means merely the creation of a new cadre of village health workers similar to the Chinese 'bare-foot doctors'; or the recruitment of traditional healers into the health system; or the setting up of vertical programmes of immunisation and oral rehydration are shying away from the main issues of equity, coverage, and the provision of basic needs. PHC is basically redistributive in character. Success of PHC requires strict control over resource allocation between sectors and within each sector. Where the political scope for reducing existing expenditure on urban hospital services is limited, PHC has tended to develop only through the earmarking of new resources, usually from outside. Countries which have used 'community participation' to extract funds, materials or labour from local communities without carrying out changes in budget allocation are in fact getting the poor to pay for their own health whilst the unequitable spending in health continues as previously. In such situations PHC may well be said to be supported in words and urban services in deeds.

A case study from **Tanzania** illustrates that change of direction towards the goal of PHC often requires courage and firm commitment. Since independence in 1961 the health services of the country had grown in an incremental manner as was usually the case in most countries. The urban bias in health services since colonial times had thus come to be accentuated. After a critical evaluation of health programmes in 1970, the budget allocation for hospitals was reduced by between 50 to 60 per cent in 1971–72, so that hospital services came to receive 20 to 25 per cent of the total health expenditure compared to 60 per cent as in previous years. During 1973–75 allocation for hospitals was further reduced to a low of 12 to 15 per cent and there was a simultaneous increase in training facilities for auxiliaries in preference to physicians and specialists. The courage in decision making and the willingness to argue out the case before the electorate can be imagined in such a situation. Health service reforms to encourage a distributive policy of the type in Tanzania are fraught with a wide variety of conflicting interests. The fact that it was achieved is an indication of democratisation of decision making, and the bridging of the social gap between the professionals and sub-professionals on the one hand, and between health service workers and the communities on the other.

PHC is thus a platform for social change as in the case of Tanzania. Besides the principle of equity in health care it identifies popular participation as an essential path for a community's health development. The responsibilities of the government in improving the quality of life of its people are stressed. The target of Health for All by the year 2000 (HFA 2000) is as much a social target as one in national planning.

In very large countries like **India** the planning process may be very complex and radical reforms are not that easy. This is reflected in the gap between intentions as described in successive national plans and reality. Hitherto all the plans have called for a rural bias, for example rural areas 'should receive much greater attention' (GOI 1952; 197);

9

they represent 'the most urgent need to be met in the second five-year plan' (GOI 1956; 534); 'the expansion will reach a progressively larger number of persons specially in the rural areas' (GOI 1961: 653); rural areas will be the 'emphasis' (GOI 1968: 309) or the 'accent' (GOI 1973: 234). Similarly a preventive bias has been urged in successive plans. Yet, the general impression of Indian health development has been the reverse of the picture as described by Indian critics as well as by outsiders (Banerji 1983; Casson 1978). The Planning Commission has been more supportive of the preventive and public health aspects of health expenditure compared to the central Ministry of Health which tends to lean towards curative facilities. Political pressures are built up resulting in the funding of medical colleges and urban hospitals because these meet the demands of the urban power groups. The State Ministries of Health are most susceptible to such pressures and the central Ministry of Health can only transmit the State proposals to the Planning Commission. In turn the Planning Commission can only restrain expenditures by State governments but cannot insist on spending on preventive programmes. The result is that the actual process of health expenditure may turn out to be different from that proposed in the plan.

However, this is not the pattern for the whole of India and some states have shown remarkable progress. In recent years the indices of health and nutrition in the Indian state of **Kerala** have shown marked improvement, surpassing some of the more well-endowed states in the country. For example, the infant mortality rate in Kerala is 55 compared to 125 for all of India; life expectancy at birth is 64 years compared to 52 for all of India; and the crude death rate is 7.5 compared to the all-India rate of 14.5. In addition, literacy rates are 69 per cent compared to 36 for all of India. All this has been achieved even though Kerala is subject to the same planning process as the rest of India. The experience of Kerala stresses the importance of regional planning in a large country like India. A number of studies have attempted to analyse the processes leading to Kerala's successes. Political changes of the fifties which helped to break the old mould led to a more redistributive approach in planning. The resulting land reforms, wage reforms, together with better security of employment for wage earning labour, expansion of education providing free access to primary and secondary schooling, access to adequate nutrition through government owned ration shops which sell grain at controlled prices, and an equitable distribution of health care have together resulted in a powerful synergism for improving the physical quality of life. Kerala is a good example of how regional or state level planning can help to turn national plans into action programmes.

The lessons to be drawn from these case studies are as follows:
1. The planning process is not politically neutral and cannot by itself bring

about rationalisation. Political systems have a strong influence in planning as in the case of Tanzania, Kerala and the rest of India.

2. Establishing priorities in health planning cannot always be in the best interests of all the groups in the country, hence the need for creating a consensus through advocacy and dialogue. The methods used will depend upon the political structure of the society, for example through the media, the political parties, trade unions, consultative committees, communal groups and so on.

3. Health planning carried out at a great physical and social distance from the mass of population can rarely be effective. Responding to the needs of the rural and urban poor requires the planning process to move nearer to them. Decentralised planning helps the resultant programmes to be more relevant to the needs of the disadvantaged than to the demands of the elite, for example the difference between Kerala and other states of India.

4. A number of factors play an overlapping role in influencing the planning process. There are the central planning body, the various ministries, the regional planning bodies together with the regional counterparts of the ministries, the private sector, international agencies and external aid donors. In Tanzania the private sector is too small to exert much influence; in Kerala it was well controlled because of political changes in the fifties, whereas for the rest of India and in many countries it can be a strong influence on planning.

Can poor nations achieve better health?

A small number of countries have achieved a remarkable reduction in levels of infant mortality in spite of low average national income per capita. These are China, Costa Rica, Cuba, Sri Lanka and as already described the state of Kerala in India. In the case of most of them a sustained political commitment to the improvement of health and welfare is the outstanding feature. Even though each country has adopted strategies unique to its situation, six common features can be identified amongst the strategies adopted as follows:

1. Long-term commitments in terms of financial and human resources were made by all the countries concerned. Even then the gain in terms of productive years of life far outweighed the expenditure. Thus the cost per year of life gained has been quite small.

2. The planning process and decision-making reflected strong concern for the health of the entire population.

3. Besides specific health programmes a variety of other approaches were used. But in all of them there was a strong element of community participation, availability of services and equity in access to services.

4. A great deal of overlap existed in the variety of approaches used.

5. Each of the approaches emphasised female education with equal opportunities for primary and secondary education for girls.

6. Much of the investment made in health went into primary health care activities as well as primary and secondary education.

A case study from **Costa Rica** illustrates the above comments. The accelerated decline in mortality in Costa Rica in the period 1970−1980 is unusual for most countries in the region. Infant mortality rate declined from 66 per thousand in 1970 to 20 in 1980 while life expectancy increased from 65 to 72 years. The dramatic health improvements in the period 1970−1980 were the result of initiatives taken during the 1970s as well as the cumulative effect of equity-oriented social policies adopted by progressive governments over a long period.

Costa Rica had reduced the infant mortality rate from 137 per thousand in 1940 to 95 in 1950. Adult literacy was already about 75 per cent in 1940 and increased to nearly 80 per cent by 1950. The absence of a military establishment enabled the state to direct resources to socio-economic development and allocate a substantial proportion of the government budget to health and education. A comprehensive social security system was established in 1942, and progressively expanded its coverage to include nearly 70 per cent of the economically active population by 1980. Large public outlays on the development of the physical infrastructure have been equitably distributed, and public utilities such as power, potable water, telecommunications, radio and television have been made available in both rural and urban areas. The proportion of the population with domestic water supply increased from 53 per cent in 1950 to 84 per cent in 1980, while the proportion served by sewage disposal increased from 49 per cent to 93 per cent.

Costa Rica enjoyed relatively rapid economic growth for three decades until the recent economic recession. Per capita incomes increased at an annual rate of 2.1 per cent during the period 1965−1983. The distribution of the benefits of growth took place largely through a welfare-oriented policy. By the beginning of the 1970s, the large majority of women entering motherhood were educated at least to the primary stage. The period of sustained economic growth, combined with equity-oriented policies, had significantly reduced the prevalence of extreme poverty and economic deprivation. The conditions were therefore conducive for a health revolution.

In the first half of the 1970s the Government took several major health initiatives: action was taken to expand the coverage of the social security services to reach the entire population; the health care system was reoriented towards primary health care; a rural and community health programme was implemented to bring health within reach of the underserved population; and community involvement in health was promoted. In 1974, the Government introduced a levy on salaries and allocated the revenues from sales taxes, under a 'social development and family subsidy' law, to finance specific health and nutrition programmes such as complementary feeding programmes. Nutrition policy decreed the enrichment of certain foods for the prevention of particular nutritional deficiency diseases. Several laws and decrees were enacted, which together with the general health law gave legal status to the health programme and defined the health entitlements and duties of individuals and institutions. In brief, the drive for improving the health status of the population became an important focus of national policy.

Reorienting the health services to support PHC

Hospital oriented services have their focus on disease. The main thrust of PHC is to distinguish health from health care of the conventional type. Since health is a product of many things, of which health care is only one, many factors in addition to health services need to be taken into account in order to improve health. Hence the need for a multi-sectoral approach so that inequalities in other services may be corrected as much as in health. Certainly at the interface between the services and the community multi-sectoral activities are necessary. The best way of ensuring it is to have community structures to integrate the inputs.

A feature of the developments in **China**, **Cuba** and **Tanzania** has been the organisation of the people through political and social change. In **Tanzania**, which has a one-party system, the party organisation works closely with the administrative system, and penetrates the community much more than the administrative system. At the grass-roots level the party representatives in the form of the village committee and the ten-house chairmen have important political and administrative roles. In addition, the women's organisation with its branches in all scattered communities has a crucial political and social role. Together they ensure that the benefits of the services are received by all and at the same time there is no abuse.

In countries with different political systems, community organisation has an even more important role because it substitutes for the lack of administative network at the periphery.

For example, in **Jamkhed** (India) the presence of farmers' clubs, women's groups and youth organisations ensures a better coverage of the programmes. In one study the use of fertilizers, high-yield varieties of seeds and improved agricultural technology was more widespread in the programme villages compared to nearby comparison areas even though governmental services were identical in both. In the latter only the big farmers were knowledgeable and used such inputs regularly. Similarly the principles of child feeding and oral rehydration were more widely known in the programme villages on account of the topics being regularly discussed by the women's groups.

These experiences illustrate an important lesson. There exist large social, cultural and cognitive distances between the poorly educated, low status population and the better-educated administrator. The administrator has a greater affinity for the elite and can be used by them to monopolise the services. Similarly, health workers may not be motivated nor have the skills to break the social, cognitive and physical barriers to reach the disadvantaged. Hence the need for community groups like those described above.

Changes required within the health system to meet the objectives of PHC

It is obvious that fundamental changes are needed at many levels in health systems to meet the challenge of PHC. Simple tinkering aided with rhetorical whitewash will not do. In a WHO/UNICEF study on national decision-making for Primary Health Care (1981) it was noted: '.. despite an internationally agreed definition, the term "primary health care" is being applied around the world to a variety of realities and even of concepts.' The study went on to state:

'... there is often a large gap between PHC plans and implementation; words abound but concrete results are thin on the ground. What progress there is seems often to be along conventional basic health service lines, sometimes extended in a cheaper version in the form of village based health workers. The scope and depth of community involvement are often doubtful. The co-ordination of health and development planning is often poor and intersectoral health-related activities are frequently rudimentary. Vertical single disease programmes are often not yet integrated with PHC in practice.'

It is necessary to examine what changes − structural, administrative and in health activities − are needed to ensure continuing progress towards PHC. Firstly, accessibility is essential. In only 66 countries (out of 166 member states of WHO) access to local health care, including the availability of at least 20 essential drugs, within one hour's walk or travel has been achieved. The peripheral sub-centre or the health-post is the front line of the health service. Neglect of these peripheral centres and their staff has been common. With a little imagination they can be changed into major staging posts for mounting community health programmes of immunisation, sanitation, oral rehydration, promotion of nutrition and so on. They can also become the

14

Fig. 2.3   The Malaysian midwife

hub of intersectoral co-ordination and community participation − two of the three pillars of PHC. Therefore in the drive towards achieving adequate coverage the structural need is for smaller health units like sub-centres, maternity centres and health posts. Since these units are largely run by auxiliaries there is a need to expand the training of such cadres through relevant training programmes. There is also the need for upgrading the skills of the auxiliaries through refresher courses, in-service training and regular supportive supervision. Such choices would require a shift of expenditure from medical schools and teaching hospitals to schools for auxiliaries, and to the building of smaller health units. How this choice was made by Tanzania has already been described.

> In **Malaysia**, an expansion of peripheral small maternity units with an auxiliary nurse-midwife in charge, and a simultaneous increase in the training of traditional birth attendants has led to a marked increase in coverage with maternity services (Fig. 2.3).

In order to overcome the isolation of hospitals from the rest of the health system it is necessary to assign a geographically well-defined catchment area to each hospital. In many cities expensive secondary or tertiary care facilities are used to provide primary care to the elite. By identifying catchment areas

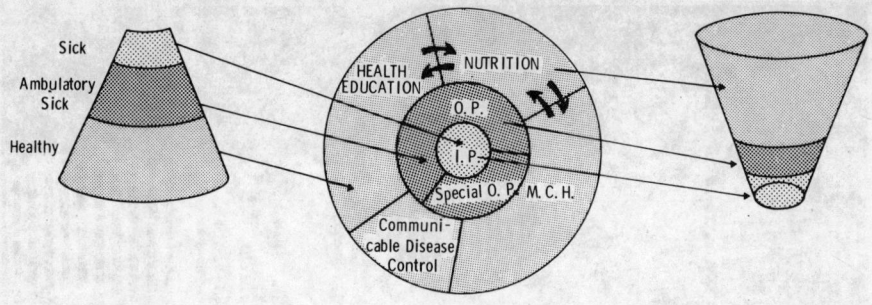

Fig. 2.4   A conceptual model of health care

and providing for adequate primary care coverage through peripheral units such an abuse can be stopped. Assignment of a catchment area by itself will not be enough unless a community health team at each hospital works closely with the staff at the peripheral health facilities and community health workers to ensure technical and logistic support as well as adequate coverage. The aim is to extend the systematic surveillance which hospital workers already provide for in-patients to the whole community − the sick, the ambulatory sick and the healthy. A major defect in all health planning (and training) is the assumption that the healthy do not need any services. In fact it is the other way round. The healthy require PHC to stay in good health. Secondly, whereas the ill may be expected to come forward for treatment because of their symptoms, services for the healthy must be delivered to them. PHC must reach out to people and families in their homes, in their places of work, in the fields, in schools, in places of worship, in the market place and so on − in fact wherever people gather. A conceptual model for such a strategy is presented in Fig. 2.4. Thirdly, the benefits of such services are apparent only when more than 80 per cent receive such services on a regular basis and when those most in need are catered for. Hence the importance of coverage and the critical cut-off point at 80 per cent. A large proportion of services which fall under PHC do not appeal to the physician or the hospital nurse because of the focus of their training and the expectations about the nature of their profession. Hence the importance of health auxiliaries and community health workers. This distinction is important. Their training should equip them for PHC work and not be stereotyped as at present aiming to produce mini doctors and nurses. It will be the responsibility of the community health team to support and help the effectiveness of such PHC workers through the use of appropriate health technology. A hierarchy of health technology can be evolved including drugs and methodologies extending from the community health workers and the medical auxiliaries to the hospital specialist.

A good example of such hierarchy of technologies is **Mozambique** where essential drugs lists of increasing complexity have been developed, extending from the level of the health post to the district hospital.

Decentralisation of planning

Being made responsible for an assigned catchment area is not by itself enough. Accountability must go along with responsibility. When hospital staff and other peripheral health workers are made accountable to distant ministries of health in countries with rudimentary postal services and other means of communication, lapses are likely to occur. It is therefore essential that health services be made accountable to the communities they serve. To achieve this a devolution of authority through decentralisation is essential. Regional and district level health committees extending all the way through to village health committees can not only ensure community involvement in health matters but also help to make constraints and shortcomings better known.

In **Tanzania** the authority of the President devolves upon the Regional Commissioner (RC) at the regional level who in turn delegates it to the District Commissioner (DC) at the district level. The administrative counterpart of the RC is Regional Development Director (RDD) who in turn has District Development Directors working under him. A Regional Development Council composed of elected representatives meets regularly to take policy decisions. The heads of the various services for example Regional Medical, Agricultural, Veterinary and Education Officers as well as the Regional Water Engineers act in an advisory capacity to the Council and the RDD within the guidelines established by their respective ministries. Thus their function is one of 'enablers' viz. enabling the people's representative to make appropriate choices, and then implementing such choices. At the grass-roots level the electoral system merges with the party system with its 10 house chairmen, and with the Regional Commissioner being the regional head of the political party. Thus, at every level there is democratisation of the decision making process. Health, as indeed all the other services, is very much part of the decentralised system of decision making, which is also more conducive to intersectoral integration.

The manner in which each country progresses towards decentralised decision making will depend upon its political culture. But as these developments occur and PHC gets established changes in the health system are likely to take place (see Table 2.1).

17

Table 2.1 Future changes in the health system for establishing PHC

	Present	Change of emphasis to	PHC supportive Health Services
What is the coverage?	< 20 per cent	→ Progressively increasing to	→ > 80 per cent
Who are currently served?	Urban and rural elites	→ Those in most need	→ Equity in provision of health care
What is the main concern of the service?	High quality care in centres of excellence	→ Provision of the eight elements of PHC	→ Preventive and promotive care for all
What are the guiding principles in planning?	International trends in the use of new technology	→ Stress on local needs	→ Epidemiological studies in the community
How is health care provided?	Through hospitals and outpatient departments	→ Development of health infrastructure for example health centres and subcentres	→ Inside the home, in villages and urban neighbourhoods
Who are the providers of health?	Specialists based in hospitals	→ Development of health teams	→ Auxiliaries, health aides and community health workers

What is the main focus of the health services?	Intensive care for in-patients	→ Concern for those who do not or cannot use the services	→ Availability and accessibility of basic services
What is the pattern of health care?	Complex care creating dependency on specialists	→ Demystification of health	→ Utilising simple technology with emphasis on self-reliance
Who are the decision makers on health matters?	Bureaucrats in distant ministries assisted by specialists	→ Increasing decentralisation	→ Community involvement and participation
What is the main thrust of research?	Bio-medical establishing the pathophysiology of diseases	→ Increasing relevance to local health needs	→ Epidemiology including social epidemiology and developing appropriate technology

Community participation

It is useful to distinguish health from health care. PHC as we have seen is proposed to act as an 'enabler'. It enables families and communities to achieve health through better awareness and by bringing together services and resources to provide basic needs and basic health care. In some situations there may be a need to mould the health system, as indeed other systems and services, to support health development at the primary level.

In the process of planning the importance of organising the people through political and social structures has been amply demonstrated.

This has been the case in **China** and **Cuba**. Similar approaches in **Tanzania** have been described in the case study on Tanzania, and also with regard to Jamkhed in India. In the Sarvodaya programme (Fig. 2.5) in **Sri Lanka** the methodologies for mobilising the population have been carefully worked out in phases. There is the initial phase of developing the *psychological base* wherein the members of the community are encouraged to develop a dialogue. This helps to generate a great deal of awareness about local problems and where they stem from. Once the psychological base has been established the next phase of developing the *social infrastructure* is begun. In this phase the community is encouraged to form several care-taker groups or committees which will serve as the supports of the programme. This is followed by the phase of the community putting up *physical infrastructures*, for example a road, a health post or a school or improved water supply and so on as the need may be. Finally there is the stage of developing the *technological infrastructure* in which the community's technical know-how is upgraded (Fig. 2.5).

In countries with socialist ideologies and one-party states the political party is the main instrument of community mobilisation. The resources and the energies of the political party are utilised for community organisation. Where the political culture has encouraged the formation of more than one party the divisions may go deep within the community and a process of dialogue or trade-offs may be needed. What must not be lost sight of are a few important conceptual barriers. Firstly, adequate diet, safe water supply, disposal of human and other waste, personal hygiene and the control of vectors and rodents are as important for health as the giving out of pills and bottles of medicines. They are also examples of activities in which the community can do much for itself. Secondly, technology is the handmaiden of the community and not the other way round. Employing a health team of outsiders to perform what are essentially community functions can only generate a dependency and a sense of helplessness. It will prevent the development of community responsibility for its own health care.

20

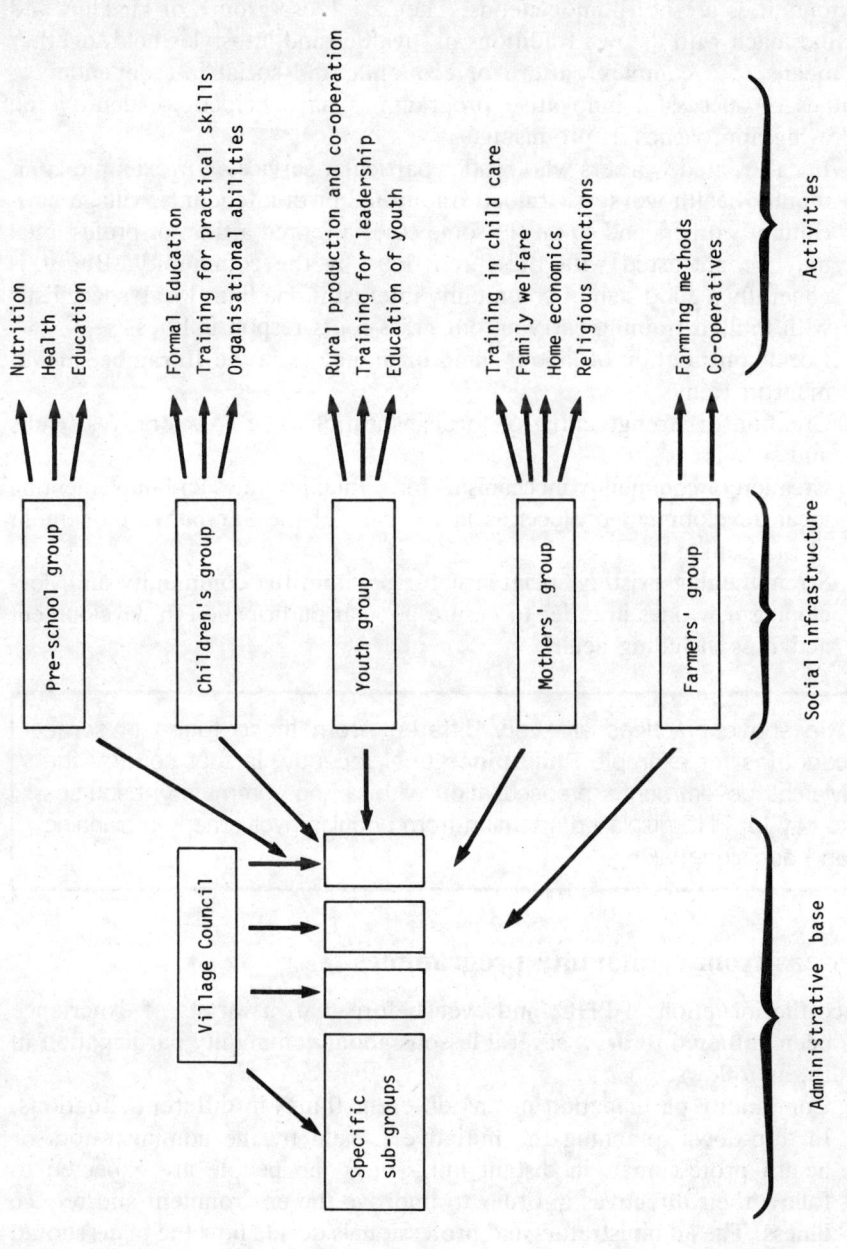

Nutrition
Health
Education

Formal Education
Training for practical skills
Organisational abilities

Rural production and co-operation
Training for leadership
Education of youth

Training in child care
Family welfare
Home economics
Religious functions

Farming methods
Co-operatives

Activities

Pre-school group

Children's group

Youth group

Mothers' group

Farmers' group

Social infrastructure

Village Council

Specific sub-groups

Administrative base

Fig. 2.5   The Sarvodaya approach to community organisation

Some successful approaches

Communities are not homogeneous. They are loose groups of kinships and families each with its own traditions of loyalties and life-styles held together by means of a complex pattern of economic and social interdependence. Studies of successful innovative programmes have helped to identify the following approaches as promising:

1. Local trained workers who render particular services, for example community health workers, trained traditional birth attendants, village agricultural workers and so on. In some cases a retired artisan or professional may be entrusted with these functions by the community. But it is generally a good sign of community interest if one finds local 'specialists' with limited training carrying out grass-roots responsibilities.
2. Local contribution of labour, land or money as in the **Harambee** movement in Kenya.
3. Creation or strengthening of local institutions like co-operatives, clubs and so on.
4. Creation of community mechanisms for setting priorities and implementing local development projects as in the case of the **Sarvodaya** movement of Sri Lanka.
5. Strengthening existing social structures within the community and developing new ones in order to ensure popular participation in development activities including health.

The above practices are very different from those found in some countries for example **Philippines** until recently. In that country the Marcos government's preoccupation with raising community resources to pay for PHC displaced attention from popular involvement in planning and decision-making.

Lessons from community programmes

Since the inception of PHC, and even before that, a variety of experience has been gathered to draw several lessons about community participation in health, as follows:

1. Community participation means different things in different situations. In 'top-down' planning the initiative is held by the administrators or health professionals in distant ministries, and people are expected to follow their directives in order to improve the environment and reduce illness. The administrators and professionals decide how the plans should progress. The people's representatives may be called in and have the preformulated plans explained without any consideration as to whether the community has adequate management structure to carry on the tasks. It is often forgotten that deprivation itself may be a great constraint

to popular participation. Those who lead a marginal existence not only lack material means to contribute but also lack education and especially time.

In the 'bottom-up' approach the professional is the 'enabler'. The emphasis is not so much on solving a health problem but encouraging change within the community as people carry out health intervention. In the words of Nyerere '. . . to plan is to choose from a set of priorities' and the job of the expert is to enable the people to reach their selected goals.

Depending upon whether the planning is 'top-down' or 'bottom-up' a variety of methods of community participation have been found, as follows:
— Programmes planned by government officials are 'explained' to local appointed leaders who help to legitimise the plans and implement them. Community councils may then be appointed through whom services and materials are channelled into the community.
— Appointed leaders from the community may be invited to attend public meetings where political leaders and officials 'explain' the plans.
— Planners come to consult with the people prior to implementation of programmes. In the light of the discussions changes may be made.
— Planners consult with the people from the beginning of plan formulation. People get a share in decision making depending upon the stage at which plans are discussed with them. People's participation in planning may be a token, and the planners remain in full control of the process.
— People have representatives varying from a handful to a full majority on the planning board.
2. Community participation is likely to be highest when activities clearly meet community needs. Health may be very low on the list of priorities, as in the case of Jamkhed where the most forcefully expressed needs were for food and water, and not for health. In a review of 35 projects around the world the American Public Health Association (APHA) came to a similar conclusion showing that there was:
   '. . . a correlation between high participation and an integrated approach open to community priorities not strictly related to health care' (APHA 1983: 47).
Hence intersectoral and broad-based activities are more likely to be successful.

Such experiences have a relevance to the style of planning. In the 'bottom-up' approach the probability of community support is greater because community needs are seen to be taken into consideration. On the other hand, in 'top-down' planning, Ministry of Health officials keen to see a policy implemented may become more involved in the technological and logistic aspects of the programme than in community participation.
3. Communities are made up of power groups with varied interests. Leaders

cannot always be expected to work in the best interests of the entire community, nor for that matter even their own group. Often new opportunities are used to further their individual or group interests. Moreover local bureaucrats or officials may have a different relationship with the landless than they do with the landowners, and a different

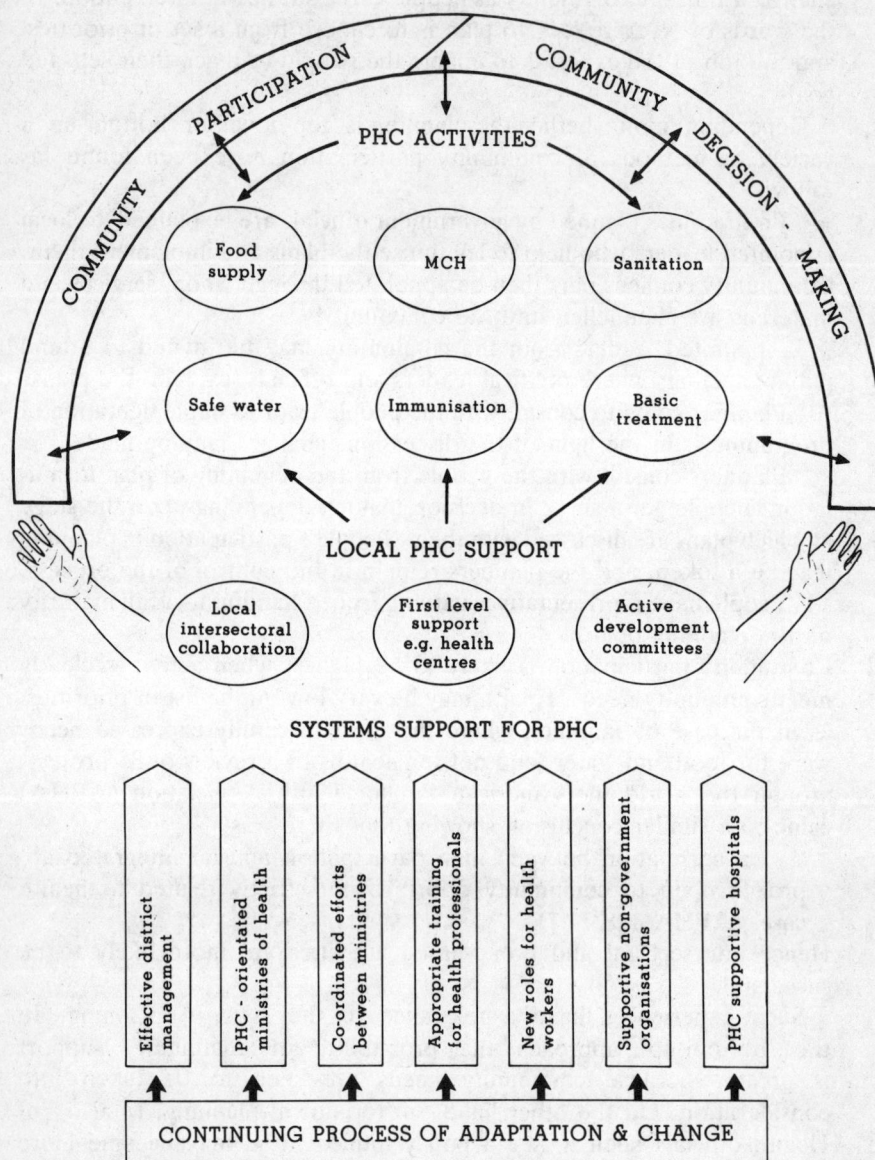

Fig. 2.6 Community participation in PHC and support for governmental ministries

relationship with workers than with the employers. Hence community participation often means readjustments in the local power structure. To look upon community participation merely as a programme element will be a mistake. Health is not a service commodity but a process of living and being. Improving health calls for change which in turn requires a number of local political issues to be carefully worked out.

There are no universal models for community participation. Factors like culture, history, political and economic background etc. largely influence the extent and quality of participation, and ways of strengthening community participation vary from place to place. It is also a dynamic process which develops further as experience accumulates (Fig. 2.6).

Reorientation towards PHC

PHC can operate in all types of socio-political systems. In any given society health improvements can be achieved through PHC without necessarily restructuring the society itself. Increments gained in health, nutritional status

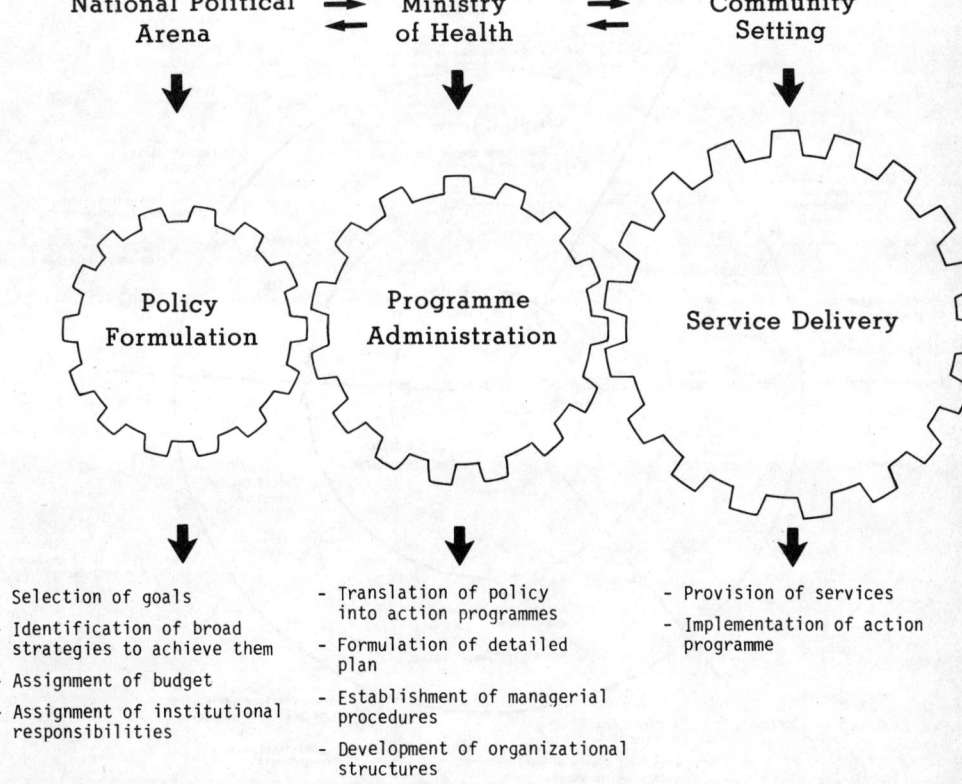

National Political Arena → ← Ministry of Health → ← Community Setting

Policy Formulation

Programme Administration

Service Delivery

- Selection of goals
- Identification of broad strategies to achieve them
- Assignment of budget
- Assignment of institutional responsibilities

- Translation of policy into action programmes
- Formulation of detailed plan
- Establishment of managerial procedures
- Development of organizational structures

- Provision of services
- Implementation of action programme

Fig. 2.7   The interlocking process of decision making for PHC

25

and knowledge need not be attained at the cost of comparable reductions for someone else.

The political issues surrounding PHC can be addressed without creating discord. There may even accrue better utilisation of resources. What is needed of course is breaking the mould of stereotyped thinking. New approaches in planning are called for which in turn must give rise to policies and strategies that would change the working of the health system. A different style of management and its support through appropriate training of health workers is needed. This calls for changes in planning, policy formulation, programme administration and service delivery (Fig. 2.7).

The national political arena, the Ministry of Health and the community setting together provide the stage for PHC. There has to be a feedback from experience. In most innovative programmes the key phrase has been 'learning by doing'. The sequence in which decisions are taken for achieving PHC are less important than the type of decisions made. There are 'political' decisions concerned with resource allocation and with distribution of authority in programme implementation. There will be 'managerial' decisions concerned

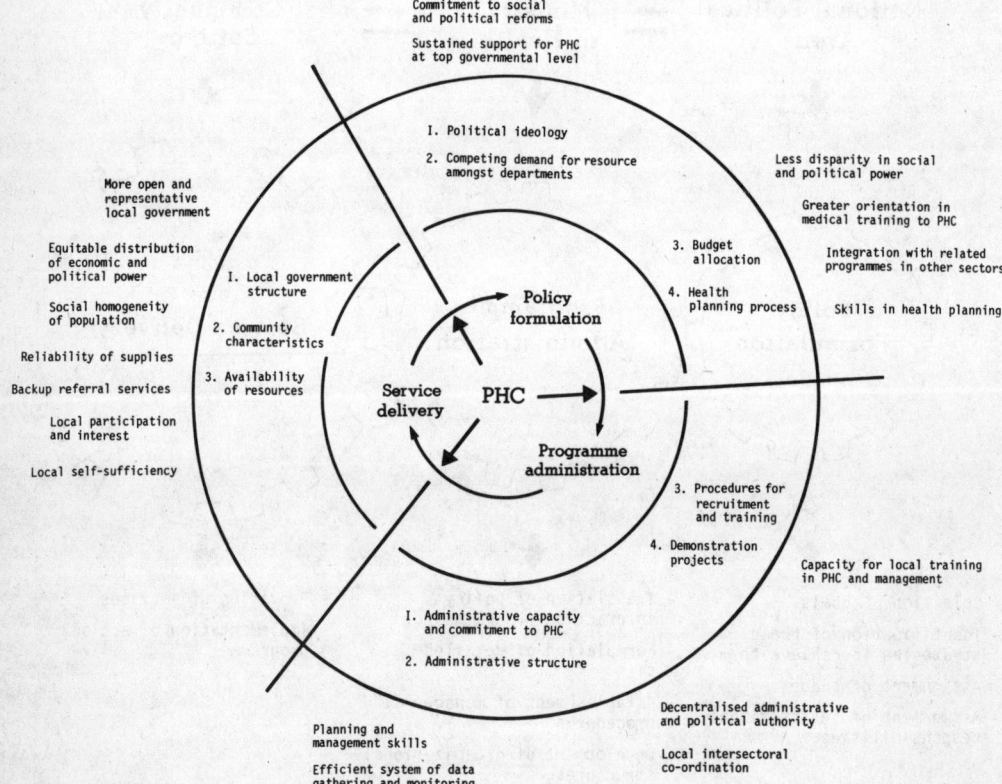

Fig. 2.8   The ingredients of success in PHC

26

with administration of programmes, and there will be 'technical' decisions concerned with the technologies to be used. Each stage of policy making in PHC is likely to be influenced by the demographic, economic and political characteristics of the country. There will also occur issues of institutional linkages, training of personnel, activities within programmes and community participation. Out of the experiences of countries several ingredients of success may be identified (Fig. 2.8). Just as the three stages of policy formulation, programme administration and service delivery are not compartmentalised but influence each other, so do the components under each heading.

Good planning requires adequate and reliable information. This is as true for those who make policy decisions as for those concerned with the delivery of services. For this both classical epidemiology which describes the Who? What? When? Where? of disease, and social epidemiology which focusses on social clustering of disease are essential. The former is needed by the programme operators and the latter is essential for planning. The social inequality in disease experience, mortality experience and of health services needs to enter popular consciousness before radical policies become accepted. This has been the case in Tanzania, Sri Lanka and Jamkhed. In a number of developing countries implementation of PHC has been attempted during periods of major turbulence including
− Wars
− Economic constraints − severe in many cases
− Political upheaval and uncertainty
− Revolution and counter-revolution
− External threats
− External manipulation − aid etc.
− Increasing poverty
− Increasing inequalities
− Mass migration including refugees
− Technological change
In such conditions, rational approaches to planned change can be virtually impossible to sustain, and there are frequent casualties in the ambitious plans of many countries.

What proves effective in such turbulent conditions is flexibility, pragmatism and adaptability provided the long term goals are clear. Formal planning may clarify some of the possible ways of achieving PHC goals but detailed plans may need to be modified or temporarily abandoned in practice. The critical skills needed are those of introducing and managing change in a specific local context and of building flexible systems which can respond rapidly to changed circumstances. In describing such organisations the analogy of the human body is still very apt − an organism capable of myriad adaptations to its environment with sophisticated but robust systems which continue to work under widely varying environmental conditions.

Change requires not only altering systems of planning administration,

27

but also introducing new systems of management. In the commercial and industrial world change has become the operative word. A number of management methods have been evolved through trial and error for managing change. Some of these methods and their application in the health field are discussed in the next chapter.

Further reading

WHO-UNICEF, Alma-Ata 1978, *Primary Health Care*, Report of the International Conference on Primary Health Care, Geneva, World Health Organisation, 1978.

World Health Organisation, *Formulating Strategies for Health for All by the Year 2000*, Geneva, World Health Organisation, 1979.

Knight, P.T. (Ed.), *Implementing Programs of Human Development,* World Bank Staff Working Paper No. 403, Washington, World Bank 1980.

UNICEF/WHO Joint Committee on health policy, *National decision making for primary health care*, Geneva, World Health Organisation, 1981.

Dean, M. (Ed.), *The Role of Hospitals in Primary Health Care*, Geneva, World Health Organisation, 1981.

Ebrahim, G.J., *Social and community paediatrics in developing countries: Caring for the rural and urban poor*, Basingstoke and London, Macmillan Press Ltd., 1985.

CHAPTER 3
Theory and Practice of Organisational Change

'When you are up to your neck in mud fighting alligators, remember — you came to drain the swamp in the first place.'
Quoted from Dr Halfdan Mahler, Director General, WHO.

In most countries, the Ministries of Health are amongst the largest employers of people. Like all organisations they exist to achieve certain objectives. The more efficient ones have precise definitions of objectives, and also have evolved systems of periodically taking a careful look ahead. Such forward looks help in the reformulation of objectives. The activities to fulfil these objectives are best defined and assigned to persons. The tasks to accomplish the activities are usually defined impersonally taking into account the relation between the tasks and the problems of their co-ordination. Having done so good management practice requires the fitting of individuals to the tasks and relating them to persons doing related tasks. Thus formal organisations define the jobs and then try to fit people as closely as possible to them.

In all formal organisations there exist problems and challenges of distribution of authority, and also those of equating authority with responsibility. If a person has less authority than responsibility efficiency can suffer. If there is more authority than responsibility to go with it then it is either redundant or dangerous. In an organisation the members of the administration are arranged in a chain of command in which the areas of responsibility and the corresponding authority diminish as one comes down the organisation from the chief executive. The specialists are not usually in this chain of command but provide a technical service to it. In such a chain of command it is usually found that for efficient working an individual should have about six and not more than ten persons working under him. In such an arrangement the organisational process which accompanies the principle of chain of command is the process of delegation. Efficient organisations encourage delegation as much as the assignment of responsibility. Delegation helps to engender a sense of responsibility amongst the subordinate staff. And this can be achieved only if they are assigned work, allowed to get on with it, and made accountable for it.

Bureaucracies and their organisation

Large bureaucracies are able to perpetuate themselves on account of three main factors. Firstly, there are fixed official duties. Work is defined methodically and distributed. Official duties carry responsibilities for getting things done. This necessitates having a certain amount of authority to impose discipline and to distribute rewards. It is important that the person in office is competent to fulfil the duties and obligations required by the office. Hence selection and training for the office is done systematically as a feature of the bureaucracy. Secondly, a system of general orders and operational procedures provides a basis for the distribution of duties and their supervision. All bureaucracies have a pyramidal structure of responsibilities and authority. Continuity is provided at the top by recruitment from below. The prospect of promotion acts as a spur for loyalty to the organisation and efficiency. Thirdly, there is a system of files and records so that know-how remains within the organisation and is not lost when individuals leave.

Large organisations are also social organisations in addition to their administrative and technical functions. Social groups form within organisations when people who work in close collaboration develop relationships beyond the formal requirements. They meet informally at work and outside, share interests and so on. As social groups form and friendships are struck they come into some form of stable equilibrium with other groups and the administrative system. The layout of the job, the formal division of labour and the personal characteristics of individuals determine the nature of the social groups. Since the administrative system is never able to control any group work in minutest detail, group controls develop within the network of the managerial control system.

Introduction of administrative change is therefore extremely sensitive work. It becomes necessary to work out the social as well as other consequences of alternative organisational arrangements before instituting them. Designing a new management structure or new working practices and introducing them as if they only had to be explained to be acceptable is likely to fail. There is a risk of setting in motion social processes leading to a breakdown of co-operation. On the other hand if there is a high level of organisational loyalty, well-developed methods for consultations and discussions, and if the general environment is such as to encourage goodwill, then co-operation may be forthcoming.

Types of change in organisations

A number of influences operate within an organisation and externally which bring about changes in its objectives and the working arrangements. There is a passive and gradual form of change which may be termed *evolutionary change*. Such evolutionary change tends to be slow and uncertain. Its effects are not necessarily helpful to the organisation in pursuing its objectives. It also tends to perpetuate what is already there with incremental additions or subtractions. Passive evolutionary change tends to discourage more radical evaluation of how well the organisation is performing; how it might rethink its objectives; the deployment of resources; structures and operating systems; roles and relationships; the relevance of services provided; and the welfare and development of the workers.

Another form of change is *imposed change*. This can come from outside, for example by a government decision to institute PHC in the country. An example of how this happened in the case of Tanzania and Kerala has been described in Chapter 2 (pages 9−10). Change may still arise from external sources which are non-governmental, for example the Sarvodaya movement in the case of Sri Lanka, and Jamkhed in India. On the other hand imposed change may be a result of internal forces, for example a small group of officials with sufficient authority and power to impose their views with or without consulting and involving in a meaningful way others in the organisation. This form of change often occurs to deal with crisis situations.

It is necessary to explore all the factors leading to change and their inter-relationships in order to *manage change* effectively. Such an analysis helps to identify those processes of change which are more useful. With a good understanding of the factors leading to change and the processes involved the implementation reduces the chance of unforeseen effects. The intended results can thus be achieved with a fair degree of certainty.

In considering the need for change and its nature as well as the processes involved, the WHEEL model depicted in Fig. 3.1 overleaf is useful. It provides the basis for a comprehensive look at the factors involved.

A simple model for the management of change

The processes involved in organisational change may be summed up in the equation $A + B + C > D$.

D represents *inertia*, the tendency for people and bureaucracies to trundle on, changing slowly as things happen to them. In such a situation change is uncontrolled. What it is and the outcome are something of a lottery!

Generally change is disliked unless people see good reason for it. New job definitions, new procedures and new styles of supervision will be subjected, individually or in groups, to the questions − Do they fit my interests? Do they offend against my values? Do they affect my future? If the answers for an individual or a group are not satisfactory it will be useless to argue that the procedures are right. Management of change therefore also requires an understanding of the social system within the bureaucracy and the tools for its analysis. Officials in power may set objectives and assign new tasks. But these directives only create the framework. They help to specify the jobs which need to be done, who will work with whom, for what purpose and under whose direction. But the way in which the framework comes to life is through the activities of individuals in their interpersonal relationships.

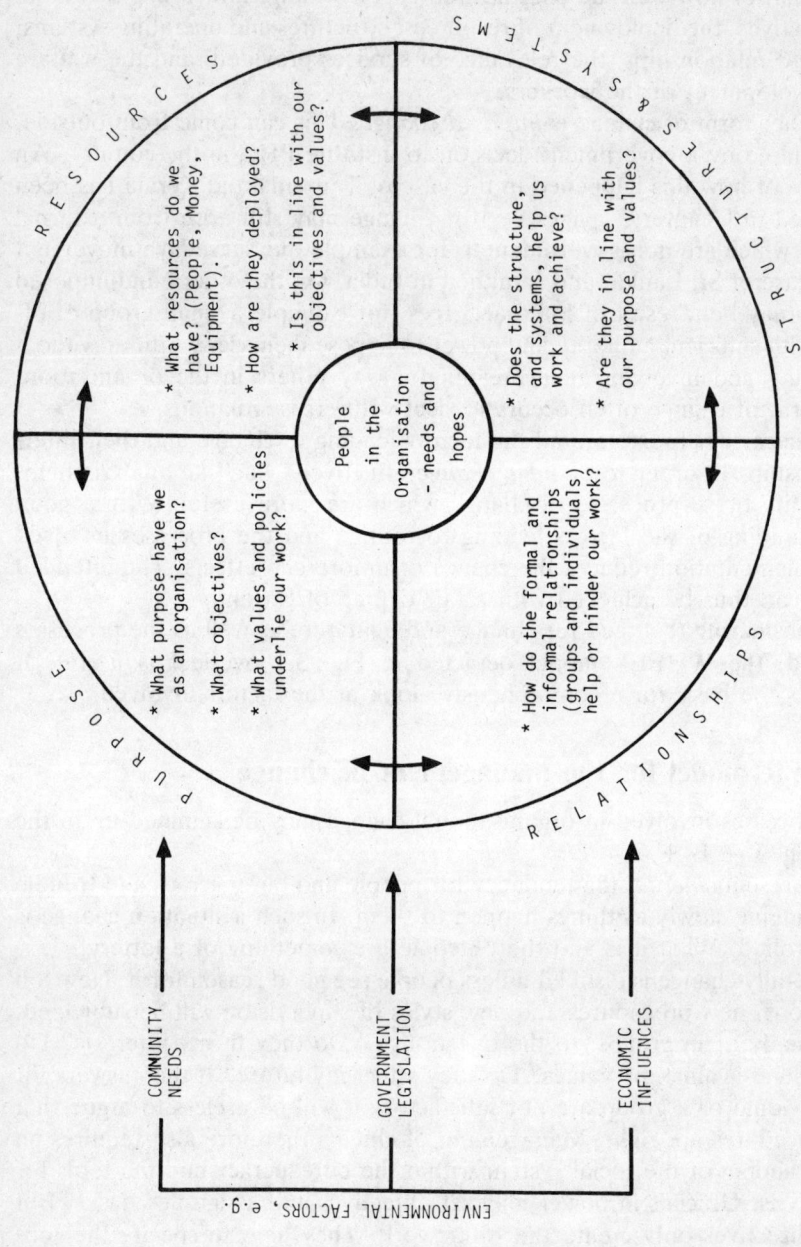

Fig. 3.1   The nature of change and the processes involved

The image contains the following labels and text:

RESOURCES
* What resources do we have? (People, Money, Equipment).
* How are they deployed?
* Is this in line with our objectives and values?

STRUCTURES & SYSTEMS
* Does the structure, and systems, help us work and achieve?
* Are they in line with our purpose and values?

PURPOSE
* What purpose have we as an organisation?
* What objectives?
* What values and policies underlie our work?

RELATIONSHIPS
* How do the formal and informal relationships (groups and individuals) help or hinder our work?

People in the Organisation - needs and hopes

ENVIRONMENTAL FACTORS, e.g.
COMMUNITY NEEDS
GOVERNMENT LEGISLATION
ECONOMIC INFLUENCES

32

Some of the reasons for resistance to change and ways of overcoming them are listed in Table 3.1.

HOW MUCH RELUCTANCE TO CHANGE IS THERE IN YOUR PART OF THE HEALTH SERVICE?
WHERE IS THIS RESISTANCE LOCATED AND WHY?

Table 3.1 Resistance to change and ways of reducing it

Reasons for resistance to change	*Ways to reduce resistance to change*
– Fear of the unknown	– Use of consultation, seminars, discussion papers, workshops, explaining reasons for change
	– Creation of shared values, ethos, greater concern for people than systems
– Loss of existing privilege	– Demonstrating that change will enhance or maintain existing status, or recompense for loss of privilege or status
– Loss of interpersonal work linkages	– Identifying efficiently working teams for assignments
– Imposed by someone else	– Look for consensus decisions / Encourage those likely to be affected to produce solutions
– Too complicated	– Keep all new procedures simple, and make adequate time available
– Increases committee work	– Reduce numbers and duration of committees
– Threat to security	– Make job requirements as consistent as possible with job expectations and aspirations
– Threat to values and ideals	– Regular training opportunities to diffuse new information and rationality
– Greater likelihood of mistakes	– Enable aspirations and expectations to be articulated
– Increase in burdens	– Informed and confident leadership

33

Dissatisfaction with status quo as the energy for change

In the equation $A + B + C > D$, **A** represents *dissatisfaction* with the outputs, for example the achievements of the service. Dissatisfaction with the results provides the energy for fuelling change. The annual reports of Ministries of Health everywhere tend to stress achievements in numbers treated, health facilities built and equipped, recruitment to the services, and so on. The issue of coverage is rarely brought up, and social inequalities in health are seldom mentioned. Such investigations and reports need to be commissioned from time to time to obtain a true picture of improvement or otherwise in the health indicators which truly matter. When people are satisfied with things as they are happening they will not be interested in change. Problems can arise when one part of a bureaucracy is satisfied and others are not.

When the energy or desire for change belongs to only part of the system it may be resented by the rest (for example the Directorate of Preventive Medicine in the Ministry of Health may be dissatisfied but the Directorate of Hospital Services may not be; or the District Medical Officers may be satisfied but people in the health posts may not be). Currently, however, there is widespread dissatisfaction in many countries with the health achievements in recent decades. This creates sufficient political head of pressure for stressing PHC in the national health programmes. When dissatisfaction is widespread, even if it varies in different grouping or levels, it provides the basic energy for change.

The 'change agent' is an example of people, either within the bureaucracy or within the profession, who are so dissatisfied with what exists that they set about creating a rationale for dissatisfaction as the first necessary element for achieving their goals.

WHAT, WHERE AND WITH WHOM ARE THE DISSATISFACTIONS IN THE HEALTH SERVICE?

Shared vision of the future

In the equation $A + B + C > D$, **B** represents a *shared vision* of the future. For example, arising out of the Alma-Ata declaration on PHC there is the shared vision of Health For All in the year 2000 (HFA 2000) as the goal to aim for. A national policy on PHC may provide such a shared vision. For example in Tanzania, the Arusha Declaration laid the foundation for the drastic cuts in curative health care and shift of resources to rural health development described in Chapter 2 (page 9). In Zambia, the main focus on Humanism provides the groundwork for the implementation of a number of programmes on human development including PHC.

Creating a shared vision sounds grand and simple but often difficult to bring about in practice. It may take a long time and involve hard work, many challenges and uncomfortable confrontations on the way. Not every manager in the health system is expected to be a visionary, nor is it always desirable! However, it is possible to identify national and international trends and pull together a group of like-minded colleagues to create a nucleus for introducing change. Examples of such international trends are the Expanded Programme of Immunisation (EPI); Control of Diarrhoeal Disease (CDD); the child survival revolution focussing on Growth Monitoring, Oral Rehydration, Breast Feeding and Immunisation (GOBI); and of course HFA 2000. A vision of a health system which is community based rather than professionally controlled may well be necessary.

A great deal of energy may need to go into creating one vision where little vision exists. This can involve meetings, seminars, workshops, seeding ideas, writing discussion papers, arguing, stimulating thinking, visits, helping people review their experience, looking at the ideas and experiences of others and testing new ideas.

It can be an exciting process and one which requires leadership, skill and persistence. If it succeeds, it provides the great strength of a unifying and motivating vision of what people actively believe in, understand and want to make happen.

It can provide understanding on what the organisation (be it the Ministry of Health, the Regional or District Health Authority or the County Health Committee) is really there to do; the outcomes that it is seeking to bring about; the values that will guide the doing of that; the ways in which it will work; how people will relate to each other; the unique and valuable contribution each makes in his own way; how it will organise a structure; the systems and efficient systems needed to support the organisation. Above all, it provides something against which, as it grows, it can measure itself.

The vision need not be totally complete (the total plan) in the beginning. After all, visions can be a little blurred and a long distance away as long as they give a clear enough future to aim for and the will to want to get there.

This discussion helps to point out that management in health services is not confined to job descriptions, promotions, settling of disputes or logistics. It is an intellectual undertaking requiring a great deal of creativity and also of evolving processes which will help release the potential of the workers. Thus the style and system of management and shared values are as important as the strategy and structure in the bureaucracy.

Incompatible visions

A difficult situation may arise when there are lots of visions which are all different and apparently incompatible. For example, to enhance national prestige it may have been decided to build grandiose speciality hospitals whereas the generally recognised need may be for the development of health infrastructure at the grass-roots level. This indeed happened during the Marcos regime in the Philippines where a number of 'organ hospitals' (for example cardiac, neurology, renal, etc.) were established in Manila.

Admittedly, such extreme situations may be less common now than some years ago but need to be guarded against. In the average situation leadership, skill and persistence are required to explore the degree of difference and the areas of shared ideas in order to build on what is shared. At times it is surprising what patience, time, skill, openness and emphasising the positive can do to create a shared vision. Such an effort pays in the end since it allows people to work effectively together whilst recognising and respecting the different views they hold.

Dwelling on the differences or emphasising them unduly, allowing too little time to explore each line of thought carefully; or tackling the differences in an off-hand manner can only cause people to dig in. Loss of face can often be a major obstacle in obtaining agreement. The people concerned become blind and deaf to the possibilities of finding some unifying agreement with others. Bureaucracies and large organisations often do not have the will, skill and time for managing change. Too often the vision comes from one group or level and is being sold to others. The ensuing discussion is largely meant for promoting and defending the vision. This process is very different from creating a shared vision. Often the 'consultation' is rushed and ends up with the active 'committee people' leaving out many who might usefully contribute and who will decide whether the changes actually work or not.

The stage of creating the shared vision is a vital one in any change process. It is difficult, complex and often time-consuming.

If, however, a shared vision is not achieved and change is proceeded with it would mean imposing one vision. Such a decision may be required on occasions and may even be a necessary reality in life. But then the accompanying reality is that people everywhere are skilled at opposing and deflecting changes which they do not really believe in.

HOW FAR IS THE VISION OF THE FUTURE IN A HEALTH SERVICE A SHARED ONE? ... WHAT MORE COULD BE DONE TO CREATE A MORE SHARED VISION?

Action plans

In the equation $A + B + C > D$, C represents knowing what the first few *practical steps* are. Even if people are dissatisfied with the existing state of the health service, and have agreed the sort of future they want to build, they will not get far if they do not know the first few practical steps needed to take them down that road.

Normally, this stage is not as difficult as the 'B' stage but it can still be a major stumbling block if a group does not possess the knowledge, skills and insights to identify those crucial steps, and/or to implement them. These first steps can be quite simple matters like:

1. Carrying out community surveys. The following questions may need to be carefully considered:

36

Do current estimates of the prevalence of disease give a true indication of the true burden of illness? Will better assessment change policy? What is the social epidemiology of disease? Will the survey and subsequent health programmes reach those most affected?

2. Finding suitable people to form action groups and committees.
3. Identifying new resources and funds.
4. Developing and running an appropriate training programme.
5. Developing efficient systems which will free and support workers, not chain them down to paper-work.
6. Improving communications and relationships between different groups of workers.

Identifying these steps and carrying them out successfully will not only take the group toward the vision, but also the success together with the learning and confidence gained from it can provide the motivation for continuing.

Even failure need not be a major setback. If every attempt is used as a learning exercise then even failures can be used for improving the design and to do better in the next round.

DISSATISFACTION + SHARED VISION + PRACTICAL STEPS > INERTIA
(A)   (B)   (C)   (D)

The culture of the bureaucracy or organisation and the process of change

One tends to speak of bureaucracies and organisations as if they were uniform in structure and styles of management. But they need not necessarily be so. In his very entertaining and stimulating book 'Gods of Management', Professor Charles Handy suggests four organisational cultures, and describes the structures and processes at work in them; the nature of power and influence in each; and their pros and cons. Normally, one culture tends to predominate in an organisation although elements of all four are likely to be found.

1. The club culture
In this type of organisation power emanates from a powerful, central leader who tends to set the style and goals for the organisation. The central figure has been compared to the mythical Greek god Zeus, the all-powerful, ruling from on high.

Procedures, job-descriptions and committees are few. These are very flexible organisations which are open to change. They are not so concerned with methods if the outcomes are good (i.e. satisfy the Zeus figure).

Obviously in such a culture, the Zeus figure will have a huge effect on the process of change. Typically, the leader's vision predominates and others accept it or get out.

Those who basically accept that vision may get close enough to help shape the vision a little and can certainly play a large part in creatively working towards it. It can be an exciting, creative, satisfying place to be — so long as you accept Zeus and the vision from on high. In many medical schools the departmental heads are often Zeus figures. Similarly, such figures are not uncommon in Ministries of Health. Certainly regional and district level medical officers often have such a style of management.

DO YOU RECOGNISE THIS CULTURE IN YOUR PART OF THE HEALTH SERVICE ? IF SO, WHERE?

2. Role culture

In this style of management there is a group of very senior people at the top who fix policy and objectives. They allocate work to people in the various divisions like Finance, Health Manpower Development, Planning, etc., which make up the main pillars of the organisation. So long as everyone does what is allotted all will be achieved in the end. The organisation is likened to a Greek temple dedicated to the mythical god Apollo with massive pillars holding up the roof. Since Apollo is the god of logic, reason rules.

Power and influence come mainly from a person's position in the hierarchy. Procedures, systems and committees are important as are job descriptions. People are not encouraged to go beyond what is laid down in the job description. It offers security, predictability in career and opportunities to develop specialist expertise within the pillars.

Organisations with a role culture may have benefits from being large. They prosper in a steady, unchanging environment. They are, however, poor at responding to market or other forces which indicate the need for change.

In many Ministries of Health there is an existing role culture with Directorates of Hospital Services, Preventive Care, Nursing, Evaluation and Planning, Training and so on. There may exist vertical programmes of Family Planning, Immunisation etc. Some ministries are in the process of adding another PHC pillar to the edifice.

In terms of our earlier 'formula' A + B + C > D, such organisations typically contain pockets of disaffection and dissatisfaction, particularly outside the most senior groupings. The structure, distribution of power and ways of working are obstacles to any open and creative process related to building a vision of the future. It may, therefore, be difficult in such organisations to talk about vision and purpose and to generate a real input from all parts of the organisation.

Change in such organisations, when it does come, is often in the form of re-organisation, perhaps with new leadership at the top. Change often focusses on new structures and systems as a way of improving effectiveness and efficiency. These changes often fail to have the desired effects because they leave the basic culture of the organisation unchanged (just substitute a new form of it) and so the old problems continue with new committees, job titles, job descriptions and new procedures for communicating and reporting.

Changing a role culture is very difficult. It often contains many people who find satisfaction in the security it offers. It can be the appropriate culture for large-scale, steady, unchanging situations.

If it is to be changed it requires coherent work at all levels and certainly requires support for and understanding of the change at the highest levels.

HOW WIDESPREAD IS THIS ROLE CULTURE IN YOUR PART OF THE HEALTH SERVICE?

3. Task culture

The task culture has a net structure, bringing together people and resources around common tasks. Teams are important. People get power through their expertise, and power is more widely dispersed in the organisation. Senior management exert control by allocation of people and resources to tasks and projects and by clarifying and getting agreement to desirable organisational objectives. Detailed supervision of method is, however, difficult. This culture is represented by the mythical Greek god Athena − the god of craftsmen and the problem solver.

This is a very attractive culture for many people, particularly those in middle positions, but it is not always appropriate and the best way of running an organisation. It tends to be unstable when, for example, there are not enough resources to go around and the common objectives begin to be lost sight of as people fight for objectives for their projects and responsibilities. In such cases the tendency is to revert to the role culture. A good example of this is when special teams are formed, for example the Expanded Programme of Immunisation.

Task culture is appropriate for many PHC support systems where there is an emphasis on teams and task groups at different levels. The task culture is more flexible and, given its acceptance of sharing, teamwork, cross-specialism and communication, it is well suited to handle the processes of change indicated in $A + B + C > D$. It still demands leadership and persistence to get it all to happen.

WHERE DOES THE TASK CULTURE EXIST IN YOUR PART OF THE HEALTH SERVICE?
SHOULD IT BE MORE WIDESPREAD OR LESS SO?

4. Existential culture

This is not really an organisation form at all. It represents a collection of individuals pursuing their own work interests. Their own objectives are more important than the organisation's but the organisation provides them with opportunities/facilities to pursue these objectives. In return, they may make some contribution to the organisation.

This culture is represented by the mythical Greek god Dionysius — the god of the individual and the first existentialist. In some countries many senior consultants and professors in medical schools are a law unto themselves. Such people often bring a great commitment to their work and, perhaps, great skill and creativity. They do, however, tend to be highly individualistic and do not fit easily into an organisation setting.

They will not easily fall in with other people's ideas but can provide useful input to the development of ideas in the change process.

Managing them is not easy both in the steady state or in a change situation. The successful engagement of such people with the organisation can be very rewarding for everyone.

WHERE ARE THE DIONYSIANS IN YOUR HEALTH SERVICE? DOES THE ORGANISATION MANAGE TO GET THE BEST OUT OF THEM?

The implications for managing change for establishing Primary Health Care

The model of A + B + C > D provides a simple framework for introducing effective change in an orderly fashion in an organisation.

The brief outline of Professor Handy's four cultures illustrates some of the difficulties in applying the framework of ideas effectively. Every organisation will tend to have its predominant culture which will probably govern the overall approach to change.

But there will probably be a mix of all four cultures and the process of managing, including change, will need to be sensitive to each and to develop approaches which are appropriate in each case.

The boundaries between the cultures are often the places where the differences are highlighted and breakdown and criticism takes place.

Positive management of these boundaries is vital for the health of the organisation. It is not enough for each culture to berate and try to impose itself on the others. This could lead to a situation likened to a 15 amp plug and a 3 amp socket — a voluntary group and a statutory body trying to do business with each other — with great pain and little success.

For those involved in the development of PHC there are a series of questions which could be useful in helping them sort out what change to bring about and how.

1. The extent How far reaching are the desired changes? Will they affect the local community or the total health care system in a country?

40

2. The organisation What is the nature of the organisation in which change is desired? Is the full organisation understood and the implications of the change understood for all aspects of it (for example using the WHEEL)? What are the best ways of trying to influence such an organisation? What is the characteristic culture of the organisation: club, role, task or existential?

3. Nature of change process Is an approach based on *managing change* appropriate? If so, where should the energy go? (e.g. in A + B + C > D terms).

Can the steps in getting a process for change started be clearly seen and linked together? How can support for them be obtained, especially at influential levels?

4. A vision Can the desired changes or the need for them be described and communicated in such a way that it stimulates and excites people? Can they become sufficiently involved to think, to take ownership of their part of the health care system, and to help shape it to be more effective?

If PHC is to change for the good then the answer to this last question needs to be yes.

Success in managing change in this way should not only produce better health for all in the present, but through experience provide people and the organisation with the understanding and learning to continue to adapt and manage change in a positive way.

The interface between the health care system and the community

A variety of local resources may be utilised to improve administrative efficiency at the local level and reduce work load. These are:

1. Utilisation of the market forces This could be the supply of nutritional supplementation through commercial outlets in Sri Lanka, or use of parastatal organisations, for example for delivery of pharmaceuticals in the Cameroon. The advantage is of low cost to the government, and quick feedback of public acceptance. The disadvantage is that the method is usually not profitable for the private sector and therefore there may be very few takers. Another disadvantage is that better off groups rather than the intended beneficiaries may profit from the method.

> This type of 'wastage' may be acceptable as a known risk, as in the case of **Sri Lanka**. Food rationing was instituted in Sri Lanka in 1943, and food subsidies for the whole population were continuously in effect for the following three decades. For the most part the programme provided cheap rice (at between 40 and 70 per cent of the market

price). In the mid-1970s one pound of rice was provided free and two were available at about 30 per cent subsidy. But in 1969–70, for each additional calorie provided to those who did not eat an adequate diet, thirteen went to people with enough to eat. More than half the benefits went to middle and upper income families. In 1979, food rations were replaced with food stamps and a poverty level was defined as annual incomes below US$ 240. However, even though only 7.1 per cent of the population lived below the poverty level almost half the population managed to get food stamps!

2. Close collaboration with voluntary agencies   These groups are characterised by strong dedication and unencumbered by top-heavy bureaucracy. Many of them have valuable experience of implementing innovative approaches, and this can be of special use. (See also Chapter 10.)

3. State bureaucracies and enterprises   are most frequently available and used. Being professionally organised and disciplined and with well-defined operating procedures which provide uniformity, predictability and account-ability they are usually the first option. But they are costly to maintain and slow to respond to non-routine questions. A World Bank study in 1979 showed that state enterprises and special authorities in predominantly agri-cultural countries had failed to promote either equity or growth in the past decade.

4. Modifications in bureaucratic structures   Some of those like decentralisation and augmenting professional staff with paraprofessionals have been well known and described on page 26. Decentralisation, in particular, allows centrally sponsored programmes to flourish under a variety of local situations. Hence adaptiveness and response to local needs is greatly enhanced.

5. Devolution of administrative responsibilities to local authorities   Unfor-tunately in many developing countries local governments are weak and inef-ficient. They can be dominated by local elites and hence faction ridden.
   Corruption also tends to be widespread. Hence training programmes for local officials are needed in order to provide a cadre of efficient managers. Regular supervision of programmes and reviews of activities are also needed, for controlling nepotism or corruption.
   Such approaches must be combined with strategies for improving the performance of the field workers. Field staff are often inadequately trained, badly supervised and poorly served by logistical and supply systems. In turn they suffer from low self-esteem. Improving their knowledge base and tech-nical skills combined with reliability of the supply system are the immediate priorities. Improving the linkages of the field staff with the formal health system on the one hand and with the community would be another objective.

In considering devolution of administration to local authorities a flexible approach is necessary. The strategy selected must take into account how weak or strong the management component is in the official health service and in the local administration. Depending upon the quality of managerial skills available an appropriate programme may then be selected as illustrated below.

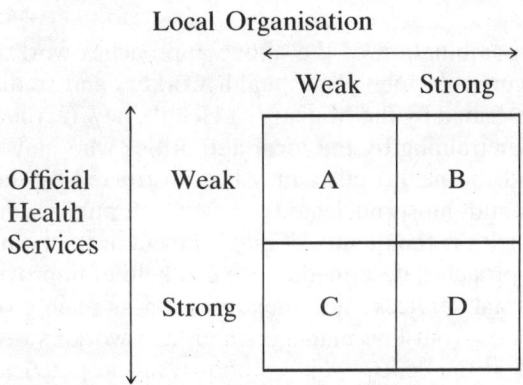

A = Where the administrative skills within the bureaucracy and the local government are poor it is unwise to initiate programmes which require either active public participation or the use of large numbers of administrative staff. In general it will also be unwise to resort to 'pilot projects' with the expectation that they will expand. Building up of administrative capabilities in the official system and locally is essential. In the meantime projects may be instituted which do not require intensive administrative back-up, for example the expanded programme of immunisation or control of diarrhoeal diseases.

D = Effective administrative systems are available to penetrate rural areas, for example in Sri Lanka, Kerala, Tanzania. In addition well organised local structures are available. Most health programmes will carry a high probability of success.

B = It may be necessary to explore ways of better utilising local government resources, voluntary organisations and people's organisations, for example Vietnam, Thailand, Indonesia. Simplicity of programme design is necessary.

C = The most suitable programmes will be those which require minimal public response, for example immunisation or basic curative services.

It is clear that often the provision of services may be a first and necessary step. Administrative systems and local institutions may then evolve around those services. For example, health services may develop and foster health committees as in the case of Jamkhed in India. These committees then facilitate the mobilisation of the people for nutrition, agriculture and development of water resources.

6. *Encouraging organisation of the people* for example Village Development Committees, Farmers' Clubs, Women's Groups, etc.

In practice a combination of the above approaches works. For example, whilst training curricula for village health workers and traditional birth attendants are prescribed by the Ministry of Health, new recruits are motivated and mobilised for training by the local authorities who may also contribute to their pay, and the health posts may be constructed by the community.

The weakest and most neglected element of public administration in developing countries is the quality of management at the point of delivery of services. The approaches described above can help to improve the quality of PHC. When formal services view their function as mainly one of 'control' the effectiveness of front-line managers and field workers declines. Administrative reforms at the centre which do not result in practical improvement at the point of delivery of service only mean a waste of resource and administrative energy. The practical actions needed are: (a) better and more relevant staff training; (b) better supervisory support; (c) improved reliability of supplies; (d) participatory style of management; (e) simplifying all procedures and (f) reducing administrative overload of field personnel.

The uptake of services at the periphery

Most of the services associated with PHC (the eight elements of PHC, page 7) require changes in the behaviour and the attitude of the user. The style of administration which responds to the needs of the users differs markedly from the 'commands' style of administration common to most bureaucracies. Moreover, the disadvantaged groups who have been largely left out of many health activities are hard to reach through the conventional systems of health care. Innovative methods for designing programmes and their implementation are needed. These may need different forms of administrative systems and structures. Ultimately the success of PHC, as indeed of any other programme, will depend upon the end-of-line fieldworkers. They are rarely motivated to break the cognitive and social barriers that separate them from their clients. The supply line to the field workers needs to be efficient and reliable.

Improving the administration at the periphery is far more complex and difficult than administrative change at the centre. The peripheral worker is also up against social and cultural factors that determine the behaviour of people, and has little training or competence in achieving behavioural change. The result is that services reach a plateau soon after they begin to function, and stay there even when inputs rise. Field workers begin to concentrate on the more progressive families in the community. Supplies start to arrive late and client response stops being fed into the administrative process. Presently very little is known of how social class, ethnicity, sex and other different characteristics of field workers and users at the community level affect their interaction.

Culture, customs and health

The kind of behavioural change required to improve public health, reduce malnutrition, control infectious illnesses including diarrhoea, rationalise home care during illness and encourage child spacing involves deep penetration into social values and culture.

Administrative change within the health system creating structural transformation may not be enough if the social and cultural values continue to remain the same. For example, the introduction of a free adult literacy programme in Malaysia did not evoke much uptake by the women who were tied down by chores at home. Low-cost community day care centres had to be set up to free young female workers from the responsibilities of child care so that they could benefit from the adult literacy programme. In Tanzania, structural change was introduced in the form of 'ujamaa' villages so as to facilitate targeting of services like health, education, sanitation and so on. But there was a great deal of resistance and even subversion when coercion was used. Subsequently the government had to accept that the value system of 'ujamaa' does not go further than the extended family. Managers are often faced with the difficult task of reconciling such cultural values of communities with the culture of organisational bureaucracy. And yet it is one of their prime tasks.

It is now commonly accepted that people resist changes which they do not understand, or which are forced on them, or which seem to threaten their cultural base. The chances of acceptance are much improved if the innovation, for example PHC, obtains legitimacy from traditionally accepted authority (for example religious or political leaders); or makes use of indigenous social structures; or is grafted onto the local cultural network. Experience has shown that the conditions for popular acceptance of an innovation are spread along a continuum, some requiring only structural transformation and others needing change in social values in addition to structural change (see Fig. 3.2 overleaf).

In one's zeal for instituting administrative and managerial change for establishing PHC it is easy to overlook the strength of the indigenous systems of socio-cultural organisation. In 200 case studies of innovative programmes failure was largely due to this cause. Any new form of service or institution replaces the previously existing one. The indigenous leaders responsible for upholding the previous form become alienated and resist the change. Hence an understanding of the indigenous socio-cultural forms is important.

45

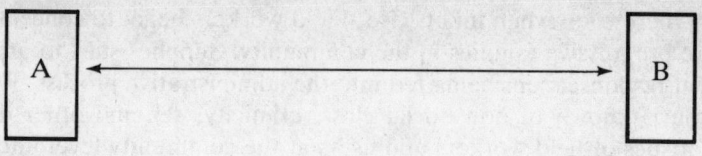

| Appropriate change in behaviour brought about mainly by providing *structural transformation* for example: land reform; minimum wage bill; food for work programmes, etc. Processes function within the existing framework of the systems of users. | Interaction between strategies of structural and value change | *Social values* must be changed through process of education; or by involving indigenous systems and institutions for example: acceptance of prenatal and maternity care; immunisation; family planning, etc. |

Fig. 3.2   Acceptance of innovation

Indigenous socio-cultural forms

Four varieties of indigenous socio-cultural network have been identified as follows:

1. Traditional leaders   Their support helps to legitimise the proposed change or innovation. Often they help the people in the process of fitting the new idea into the existing socio-cultural framework, hence the advantage in training and recruiting traditional healers and birth attendants.

2. Traditional communication systems   In the illiterate society information travels by word of mouth. Balladeers, song-and-dance teams, puppeteers and shadow theatres play a useful role in the transmission of information besides providing entertainment. Their recruitment for providing health information is a way of adapting local cultural forms for transmitting new knowledge. In this way local culture can be a help rather than a hindrance to change. A modern development of such a communication system is the radio forums and discussions groups so well utilised in Lesotho and Tanzania for distance learning.

3. Indigenous organisational forms   In many cultures indigenous organisational forms exist to deal with community problems, for example *gothong royong* in Indonesia, self-help (Harambee) groups in Kenya, rotating credit associations in many parts of West Africa. Such institutions can be further developed to provide linkages between structures inherited from the past and building for the future.

4. Indigenous knowledge systems exist which remain unknown to the city-bred official. Knowledge of agricultural methods, medicinal plants, availability of underground water, etc. are all examples of such knowledge systems.

The amount of resources needed for changing health coverage from not more than 20 per cent to 'Health For All' is so massive that a significant proportion must be mobilised outside the conventional budgetary system. A good insight into non-conventional administrative resources as well as the indigenous socio-cultural systems will help to create a useful blend of local initiative, locally mobilised resources and indigenous leadership for the PHC initiative.

The management of change in the health systems for orienting them towards PHC requires not only administrative changes within the bureaucracies but also the following strategies for reaching all the groups:
1. Extensive use of local social organisation. If local social institutions do not exist informal networks can be used and later developed into more formal associations.
2. Self-help and similar activities which increase community participation and also mobilise resources.
3. Programmes presented through the indigenous socio-cultural systems, for example religious or traditional leaders are likely to be more credible.
4. Radio forums and listening groups which can be effectively utilised for putting over the health message.
5. Strategies which are compatible with the local cultural pattern.
6. Health service activities which fit with the community's work patterns.

In conclusion, management of change within the organisational bureaucracy must extend beyond the formal health system for utilising non-conventional administrative resources. It must work within the indigenous socio-cultural framework. Then only truly participatory forms of management systems can be created for sustaining PHC in the long term.

Further reading

Kanter, R., *The Change Masters*, London, Counterpoint, 1983.

Handy, C., *The Gods of Management*, London, Pan Books, 1983.

Katz, D. and Kahn, R. L., *The Social Psychology of Organisations*, Chichester, Wiley, 1966.

World Health Organisation, *Primary Health Care: the Chinese Experience*, Geneva, WHO, 1983.

Gish, O., *Planning the Health Sector: the Tanzanian Experience*, London, Croom Helm, 1975.

CHAPTER 4
Ministries of Health and Primary Health Care

'..... It calls for organisation and strengthening of health infrastructure based on primary health care, and for health manpower
policies which will not only provide training and motivation and
ensure equitable distribution of human resources, but will also
ensure the development of managerial, technical and scientific
staff at least to the critical level of competence.'

World Health Organisation. Seventh report of the
World Health Situation 1986; page 28

Primary Health Care (PHC) is both an approach as well as a concept. As an
approach PHC places emphasis on comprehensive (curative, preventive,
promotive and rehabilitative) health care, which should be developed with
the population even in the remotest areas of the country. As a *concept*, PHC
places emphasis on several health related activities (such as nutrition, sanitation, housing, safe water supplies etc.) many of which are outside the
traditional responsibilities of the Ministries of Health (MOH). Further,
PHC will be successful only if it is integrated with socio-economic development of the population, with maximum individual and community self-
reliance and participation.

All member countries of the World Health Organisation (WHO) have
affirmed the intention to attain the goal of Health for All by the year 2000
(HFA 2000) with PHC as a tool for the provision of health services to the
under-served. There is a growing awareness of the need to reorient health
systems to PHC as a critical element in reducing inequality in health care.
Ministries of Health in developing countries have also formulated national
policies, strategies and plans of action for achieving the goal. Many countries
have restructured or reorganised the Ministries of Health; have established
co-ordinating mechanisms within the health sector and have expanded the
health care delivery structure. However, it is comparatively easier to
lay down the policy, strategies and plans than it is to implement. This is
more difficult in the case of PHC, the implementation of which crosses the
conventional boundaries of the MOH.

48

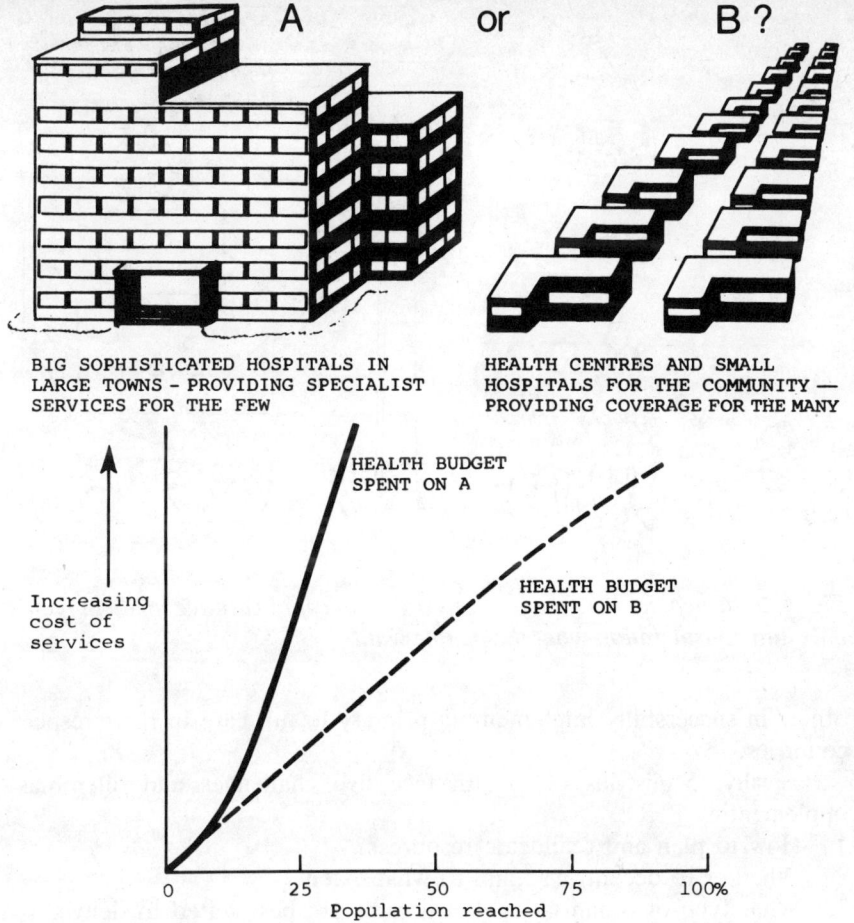

BIG SOPHISTICATED HOSPITALS IN
LARGE TOWNS – PROVIDING SPECIALIST
SERVICES FOR THE FEW

HEALTH CENTRES AND SMALL
HOSPITALS FOR THE COMMUNITY —
PROVIDING COVERAGE FOR THE MANY

*Fig. 4.1   Imbalance in present investment in health services. Cost increases
with specialisation*

To support PHC, Ministries of Health have to reallocate their resources
and also reorient and reorganise existing management structures. Thus,
adherence to and operationalising PHC has implications for the MOH both
internally and externally. *Internally*, in addition to the implications for
organisation and management, the MOH has to change traditional attitudes
of professionals and bureaucrats. *Externally*, Ministries of Health face
challenges from other Ministries as well as consumers. The achievement of
health goals is largely determined by policies that lie outside the health
sector and in particular by policies aimed at universal access to health,
education, provision of basic needs and earning a livelihood.

The present chapter looks into how Ministries of Health in different
developing countries are meeting this challenge. The positive and negative
experiences of various Ministries of Health may be useful guidelines for

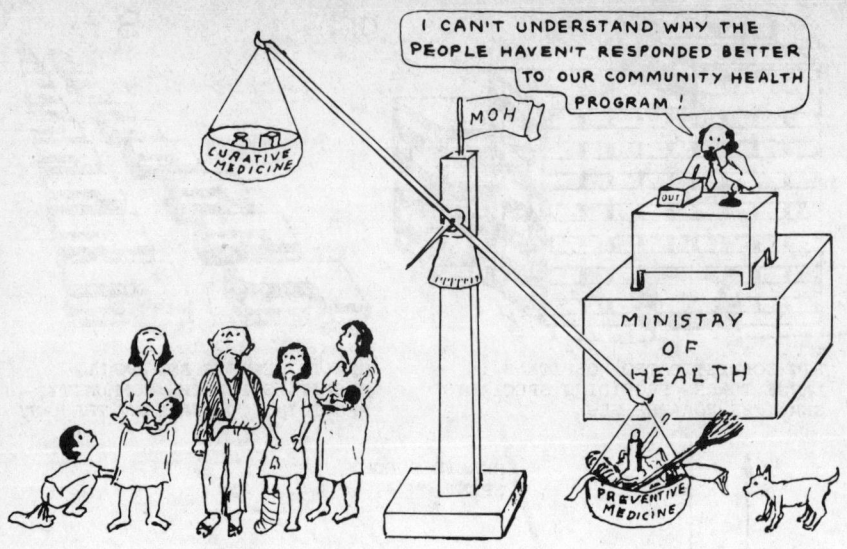

Fig. 4.2   A healthy balance between preventive and curative medicine must take into consideration what the people want

others in successfully implementing primary health care in their respective countries.

Basically, Ministries of Health face five challenges and dilemmas in implementing PHC:
1. How to plan and reallocate resources?
2. Whether to decentralise and to what extent?
3. What type of organisational structures are best suited to deliver PHC effectively?
4. How to promote inter-sectoral co-operation and collaboration?
5   How to promote community participation?

Health planning and resource allocation (Figs. 4.1 and 4.2)

We have already mentioned that many factors such as safe water supplies, housing, education, food etc. are outside the control of the MOH, but are important for better health. This brings the need for intersectoral planning. Further, PHC is not a cheap health option. Significant resources are required for it. These can be achieved in developing countries by a reallocation of available resources between competing governmental sectors. Resources will need to be allocated within a different set of health priorities from what has been customary in the past. In fact, reallocation decisions are the real test of the commitment of policy makers to implementation of their stated policies.

However, as regards health planning, experience shows that in many developing countries it concentrates on the existing programmes of the MOH; or on how to use any development money for new services or projects. Health planning being a new phenomenon, Ministries of Health are still relatively weak in planning capabilities. Further health planning has few or no links with developmental planning and is usually carried out in relative isolation within the MOH. Similarly, the allocation of resources follows the previous pattern. Little attempt has been made to reallocate funds within the health sector itself, except in a few countries like China, Sri Lanka, Tanzania and so on. Moreover, the health planning process is top-down and is a patchwork based on the recommendations of various committees.

For example, in **India**, health planning is based on the work of various technical committees appointed by the Government of India to study the problems of health in the country. Also, the Health Plan is a part of the overall National Plan prepared by the National Planning Commission. It is no more than a collated plan. Various sectoral working groups, made up of representatives of the relevant central and State Ministries, National Planning Commission, State Planning Boards, and outside experts, prepare sectoral drafts, which are then collated, compared and modified. The process has led to plans which give varying degrees of priority to health and health related sectors. Table 4.1 shows Health and Health-related Outlays and Actual Expenditures as a percentage of total public sector plan under various Five Year Plans of the Government of India. It is clear from the Table that the decline in percentage allocation to health has been compensated by a rise in outlays in the health-related sector. One may also observe that the actual expenditure is less than the outlays in both the sectors.

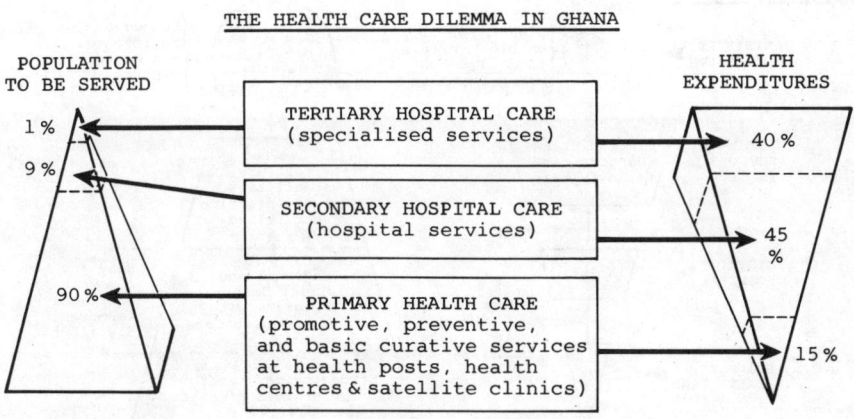

Fig. 4.3   The health care dilemma in Ghana

51

Similarly in **Pakistan**, the Federal Planning Commission has overall planning responsibilities. Within the Planning Commission, the chief of the Health Section has the responsibility for health planning. With some notable exceptions (for example the recent funding of a national programme of immunisation by delaying building plans for a major specialist hospital), the MOH remains incapable of controlling the expansion of medical training and maintaining the balance between primary and secondary care. The allocation of resources still favours federal and provincial levels. The pattern of the recurrent and maintenance expenditures on health in urban and rural areas is also unbalanced. It is noted that 50 per cent of capital expenditure was still on hospital beds, medical education and research. Such a dilemma is common and Fig. 4.3 is an example of the expenditure pattern in Ghana.

As distinct from the top-down process of health planning in India and Pakistan, a combined bottom-up and top-down process has been tried in **Mozambique**. Though overall decisions about plans are made by the National Planning Commission, the more peripheral levels are also expected to play a significant role in the planning process. Before the plan matures to its final stage, there is much activity peripherally. In general, broad guidelines are developed at the centre, which are treated as a constraint by provincial and district authorities in producing their local plans. Each sector, including health, develops its proposals for the districts, which are collated at the provincial level to give a provincial sectoral plan. This results in interactions between higher and lower levels and different sectoral plans.

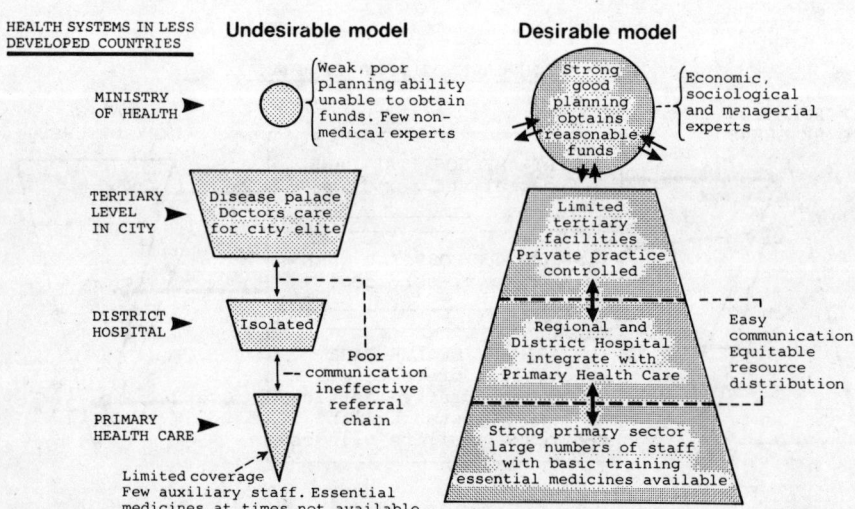

Fig. 4.4   Towards appropriate structures for PHC

TABLE 4.1 *Health and health related outlays and actual expenditures under various five year plans, Government of India (as percentage of total public sector plan)*

	HEALTH		FAMILY WELFARE		WATER SUPPLY and SANITATION		TOTAL	
	Outlay	Actuals	Outlay	Actuals	Outlay	Actuals	Outlay	Actuals
First Plan 1951–56	3.6	3.3	0.03	–	2.0	0.56	5.63	3.86
Second Plan 1956–61	3.3	3.0	0.07	0.1	1.7	1.58	5.07	4.68
Third Plan 1961–66	2.8	2.6	0.4	0.3	1.4	1.2	4.6	4.1
Annual Plan 1966–69	–	2.1	–	1.1	–	1.6	–	4.8
Fourth Plan 1969–74	2.7	2.1	2.0	1.8	2.6	2.9	7.3	6.8
Fifth Plan 1974–79	1.7	1.9	1.3	1.3	2.5	2.8	5.5	6.0
Plan Holiday 1979–80	–	1.8	–	1.0	–	3.2	–	6.0
Sixth Plan 1980–85	1.8	1.9	1.0	1.0	4.0	3.6	6.8	6.4

Source: Government of India – Plan Documents   Government of India, Ministry of Health and Family Welfare
Directorate General of Health Services, Central Bureau of Health Intelligence

In general, it is found that irrespective of claims made by the various Ministries of Health in developing countries, these plans are still dominated by a professional bias. Planning capacity is weak. The best way to rectify this situation is to establish a health planning unit within the Ministry of Health or strengthen the existing one with skilled and trained staff. The unit should be given full support and importance by the MOH. Externally, the MOH should work for creating a sympathetic and knowledgeable group in the government planning machinery including the Ministry of Finance. Such a move would strengthen the position of the MOH and argue for reallocation of capital and recurrent budget in favour of PHC. The MOH should also develop a mechanism for bottom-up planning, for which decentralisation is essential. Fig. 4.4 identifies the existing weak links in the organisation of health services and suggests ways of strengthening these links.

An important factor determining planning is the way PHC is perceived. Many countries still view it as a method of extending basic health services especially to remote rural areas. Others perceive it as a way to mobilise the community as an equal partner in the development process. The approach to national health planning is often a reflection of such views.

The above experiences point out clearly that before embarking on decentralisation, it is important that the MOH should have a sufficient number of appropriately trained health planners, administrators, and district medical officers with broader understanding of management and the implications of PHC. The issue is also very sensitive politically and needs careful handling (Fig. 4.5).

Organisational structure

PHC requires a dynamic approach and its successful implementation envisages

WHEN FACED WITH SENSITIVE POLITICAL
OR SOCIAL ISSUES AFFECTING HEALTH,

DON'T STICK YOUR NECK OUT
UNNECESSARILY,

BUT DON'T HIDE YOUR HEAD
IN THE SAND EITHER.

In the long run, one way can prove as dangerous as the other.

Fig. 4.5   The dangers of dealing with sensitive issues

a change in the traditional organisational structure of the MOH. In general Ministries of Health still follow a common administrative pattern – the Health Minister, the Permanent Secretary or equivalent and series of grades of medical and non-medical functionaries with fixed relationships and responsibilities. Different functional divisions are responsible for curative and preventive health care. In some cases, under pressure, ad-hoc changes have been made in the existing organisation of an MOH, for example by adding a division of Rural Health (see organisational chart Fig. 4.6 – India) or for Basic Health Services (see organisational chart Fig. 4.7 – Pakistan). This leaves the basic power structure in the MOH unaltered.

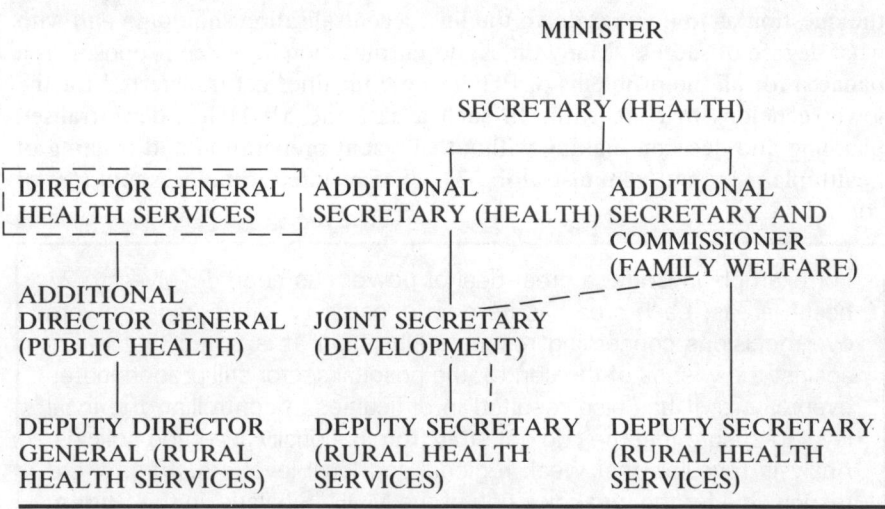

–– shows reporting and advisory relationships.

Fig. 4.6 Partial organisational chart – Ministry of Health and Family Welfare, India

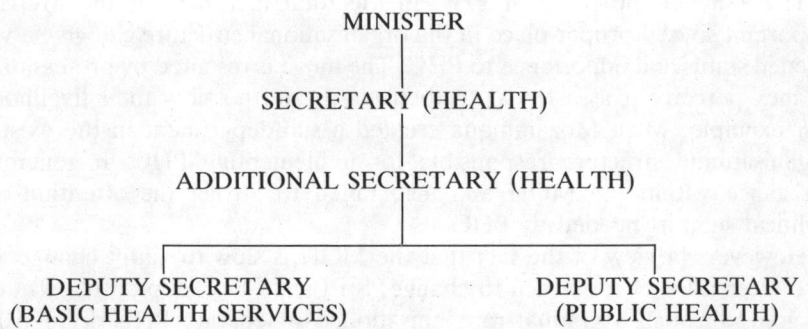

Fig. 4.7 Partial organisational chart – Ministry of Health and Social Welfare, Pakistan

Decentralisation

Once health policies and plans have been laid down, Ministries of Health face the challenge of implementing them effectively. The method suggested for this purpose is decentralisation. It is desirable not only because it helps in implementing broad centrally agreed policies, but also because it can respond to local needs and cope with the often unpredictable changes in circumstances affecting the peripheral areas. It also encourages decision-making and accountability at the grass roots level.

Decentralisation entails the delegation of power to lower levels of the political system such as region, provinces, districts, etc., but has wider political overtones. Besides being important to the MOH internally, the MOH faces the question as to how far down the line decentralisation should go and with what degree of success. Many times, decentralisation has been proposed as a panacea for all the problems of PHC. The difficulties get transferred for the lower echelons to cope with. In such a case the MOH has decentralised planning and decision making without sufficient preparation and training of health planners and administrators. This has resulted in failures and loss of control.

> For example in **Chile**, a great deal of power has been devolved to 27 health areas; each area has its own director, who has wide powers over decisions concerning resource allocation. It is noted that much against the wishes of the centre, the hospital sector still predominates everywhere. It has also resulted in difficulties in controlling the local level to ensure that they do not stray from nationally accepted policies. Analysis revealed that weak regional and local level structures were responsible for the weak position of the MOH. Similarly, in the **Sudan**, the MOH has given considerable freedom of decision making at lower level; yet, it failed to bring desired results and many districts still favour hospitals as against PHC.

The issue of the place of PHC in the total hierarchy of the MOH is important since a proper place in the organisational structure can give a well needed status and importance to PHC. The move is resented by professionals as they perceive it as a threat to their status and possibly their livelihood. For example, when Mozambique created a sub-department in the existing organisational structure responsible for implementing PHC, it generated resistance within the MOH and also failed to attract the attention and political support needed by PHC.

However, in view of the fact that the MOH is slow to adopt change and also faces a lot of resistance to change, Sri Lanka has adopted the strategy of going through a gradual reorganisation. No separate PHC division has been created. This has reduced the resistance in the MOH. Efforts have been made to infuse the MOH with the spirit of PHC. The government is

56

working on solving problems of co-ordinating PHC related activities with preventive health services, shifting of resources towards PHC and division of responsibilities between district development councils and the centre.

For successful implementation of PHC, proper organisational structure is important at the centre as well as at the intermediary and local levels. Often PHC programmes have been launched by the MOH without creating a proper organisational structure and without training at the district and local levels, which results in poor performance.

For example, in the **Philippines**, a multisectoral structure has been created to promote and direct PHC activities. It involves committees and officers both in the MOH and in other sectors at all levels. There is a National PHC Committee in the Ministry of Health, with representatives from other main ministries concerned. A Technical Working Group is chaired by the PHC Co-ordinator, who is a senior official and reports directly to the Minister. This assigns a high status to the official as well as PHC. Similar committees and officers are assigned at regional, provincial and municipal levels. At national and provincial levels, the committees are working well. But, performance is not good at regional and local level because of organisational unpreparedness and lack of training.

Thus, whatever form of organisational structure is created by the MOH, timing is important. Change which is gradual may generate less resistance. On the other hand, there is sometimes a case for making changes boldly

'THE TWO MULES'

A fable for the Nations

CO-OPERATION

IS BETTER THAN CONFLICT

Fig. 4.8   Success through co-operation

where the change is important and has senior level support. Further, proper organisational mechanisms and structures should also be developed at the regional, district and local levels. These should be staffed with properly trained personnel having adequate authority and control of resources, full support and supervision.

Intersectoral co-operation and collaboration

Where the PHC approach as a means of achieving Health for All by the year 2000 has been adopted by a developing country, it is logical for the MOH to seek co-operation from the non-health sectors. However, in view of the long history of isolation of the health sector as well as its low status among the various Ministries, the task is not an easy one. Further, there is also a common belief that the health sector is a 'bottomless pit' which consumes resources but makes little contribution to development. The Ministry of Finance may block any effort on the part of MOH to implement PHC because it is unaware of the importance of PHC. Lastly, within the health sector itself there may be strong resistance among professionals to the idea of non-health sectors becoming involved in matters of health.

To meet this challenge, the MOH can take actions internally as well as externally. Internally, a change within the organisation can provide support for intersectoral linkages. For example, different departments may be given responsibility for linkage, or jobs may be defined in such a manner as to encourage liaison with other Ministries. However, joint programmes may be successful only where all the participants are not influenced by sectoral interests. Ministries of Health are still searching for mechanisms to accomplish this internal change, which may not be possible until other Ministries collaborate willingly and closely.

Externally, at national level some form of mechanism for intersectoral interaction (not co-operation and collaboration) does exist in some countries. For example, in India, some intersectoral contact takes place as a matter of routine in the National Planning Commission, but there is no evidence of intersectoral collaboration after the planning process at the national level.

Depending on local circumstances, a strong case can also be made for placing responsibility for co-ordinating PHC outside the Ministry of Health, for example in the Cabinet Office or Office of the President. This can demonstrate high level commitment to PHC, and also secure the involvement of Ministries which do not see PHC as a high priority.

A partial success story in relation to intersectoral co-operation comes from the **Philippines**. There a multisectoral organisational structure has been put together in order to promote and direct PHC activities. It involves both the MOH and other sectors at all levels from the centre to the village, as part of the intersectoral development committees/ councils. At national and provincial levels, the committees are working quite well. However, the report from the local level is not encouraging.

Another good example of intersectoral collaboration comes from **India**. In order to meet the health needs of a growing population in urban squatter settlements and the remote rural areas, the government of India launched a programme of Integrated Child Development Services (ICDS) in 1975. The objective of the scheme is to reduce the incidence of malnutrition and child mortality amongst the poor communities. ICDS aims at providing a package of services to preschool children, pregnant women and nursing mothers. The services include supplementary nutrition, immunisation, health surveillance, health education, non-formal education and referral. The ICDS programme is implemented by the Department of Social Welfare in collaboration with the Ministries of Education, Health and other related Ministries. The administrative and service framework of each project covers one block, and the programme is being extended to cover 1000 blocks.

The MOH can take assistance from International aid agencies, particularly those contributing to health-related sectors such as agriculture and education. Their assistance may be sought firstly to encourage the recipient governments to establish mechanisms for intersectoral action, particularly in planning for health; and secondly, to ensure that their own departments co-ordinate their activities to achieve maximum benefit for health development.

However, the onus to stimulate interest and promote intersectoral co-operation and co-ordination is on the MOH. It needs to be alert and innovative and should capitalise from any opportunity for intersectoral co-operation and co-ordination.

Community participation

Community participation is used loosely for different PHC activities which are related to the economic, learning and political spheres. The economic dimension of community participation is related to the contribution of resources (materials, labour and money) to health-promoting activities. It also relates to enlisting support from the community to carry out certain tasks, for example, the village health worker scheme. In terms of learning, community participation is a two-way process involving both community members and health workers. Here, community and health workers learn from each other. Finally, community participation is a political process as community members acquire a say in decision-making about health and health related issues that affect them. There is an awakening and the community starts to question how things are done, and why the health services have not been organised and managed effectively to meet their needs. They may point out new methods of solving the problems, which may not suit the ways of the MOH and even the political system. Community participation in this sense raises organisational problems for the MOH as well as for the political system.

Fig. 4.9   The disciplines which need to work together for health

So far the MOH have made attempts in two directions. Firstly, Ministries have enlisted the help of community members to carry out health-related tasks at the grass roots. These community members are recruited at local levels, work part-time or are trained traditional birth attendants. But experience shows that often this type of community participation creates more problems than help. For example, in India, village health workers have been recruited and trained under different and changing names. The programme has run into difficulties because of culture, caste system and resistance from professionals. In Turkey and the Yemen Arab Republic, community participation has been limited to donation of materials, labour and construction of facilities.

Secondly, where traditional forms of decision-making at local level exist, Ministries have taken steps to revive the system. In Ghana, efforts have

Fig. 4.10   Two attitudes to health care

been made to mobilise the community through traditional forms, facilitating the setting up of a health committee. The Philippines and Sri Lanka have similarly encouraged the formulation of village development committees.

Countries with large rural populations have long-standing traditions of community participation in local development activities. Many of these cultural traditions are proving to be of great value in PHC activities. Wherever progress has been achieved in community participation it has been largely through utilising existing traditional mechanisms; for example, in the tradition of *Gothong royong* in Indonesia villagers may help one of their number after normal work. This tradition has been utilised for setting up community reliance institutions (the 'LKMD'). Mothers' groups have been used for regular weighing sessions for children to monitor their growth.

The above examples indicate that in many countries only rudimentary efforts have been made to encourge community participation. This may be because the spirit and meaning of community participation is not fully understood, or alternatively because courage is lacking to meet the challenges which the organisational, managerial and political issues of community participation will impose. In both cases, the MOH should accept the reality. There is no universal solution in this complex area of political, social, and organisational change. Each country has to find appropriate solutions. It is for the MOH to develop an approach most suited to local needs.

To sum up, Ministries of Health in developing countries have adopted the concept of HFA 2000 and also formulated national health policies based on the PHC approach. However, Ministries are faced with the challenge and dilemma of implementing the national health policy with limited resources. It demands an innovative approach at political, professional, economic, social and cultural levels. In doing so, Ministries need to change internally

? Where do we start building the pyramid of health care

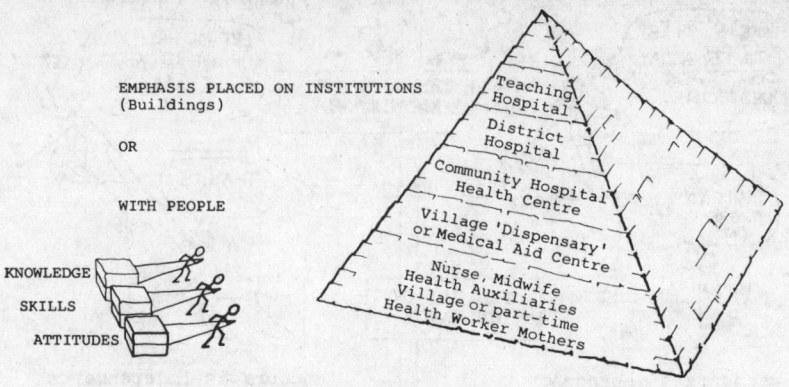

EMPHASIS PLACED ON INSTITUTIONS
(Buildings)

OR

WITH PEOPLE

KNOWLEDGE

SKILLS

ATTITUDES

Teaching Hospital
District Hospital
Community Hospital Health Centre
Village 'Dispensary' or Medical Aid Centre
Nurse, Midwife Health Auxiliaries Village or part-time Health Worker Mothers

Fig. 4.11   Where do we start building the pyramid of health care?

and externally. The practices adopted and lessons learnt by other Ministries of Health as well as modern management concepts will also be useful to meet this challenge. As current global thinking favours the PHC approach, there will be popular support for MOH policies in that direction. What is required is a strong determination and the creation of appropriate structures within Ministries of Health to carry out the necessary changes.

Further reading

Kleczkowski, Bogdan M., Roemer Milton I. and van Der Werff, Albert, *National Health Systems and their Orientation towards Health for All — Guidance for Policy-making*, (Public Health Paper 77) World Health Organisation, Geneva, 1984.

Rondinelli, Dennis A., Nellis John R., Cheema, G. Shabbir, *Decentralisation in Developing Countries — a Review of Recent Experience*, The World Bank, Washington, 1984 (World Bank Staff Working Paper, No. 581).

Rifkin, Susan B., *Health Planning and Community Participation — case studies in South-East Asia*, Croom Helm, UK, 1985.

Government of India, Planning Commission, *Seventh Five Year Plan — 1985—90*, New Delhi, 1985.

Government of India, Ministry of Health and Family Planning, *Annual Report 1984—85*, New Delhi, 1985.

A Report on the Pyongyang Conference on Primary Health Care in Action, World Health Organisation (Regional Office for South-East Asia, New Delhi, 1985.

Report Seven, Commonwealth Health Ministries Meeting, 1983, Commonwealth Secretariat, London 1984.

World Health Organisation, *Strengthening Ministries of Health for Primary Health Care*, WHO Offset Publication No. 82, Geneva, 1984.

CHAPTER 5
Strengthening District Management

> For the delivery of Primary Health Care countries have to be divided into manageable units — geographical areas small enough to be managed without sinking in the mud of central bureaucracy yet large enough to make it feasible to include most of the ingredients required for self-reliant health care.
>
> Halfdan Mahler, Director General,
> World Health Organisation

There is a growing consensus that an effective system of Primary Health Care at the national level will grow out of effective district PHC. In many government health systems the district, with populations of around 200 000, is the key intermediate level of health care delivery, its management and co-ordination. Whilst implementing national policies and programmes it is small enough to be close to local communities and to reflect their needs. As the basic administrative unit it acts as a link between local government, other government departments and non-government agencies. In a typical health district there will be a network of smaller health units providing basic services and supporting community based activities, with secondary services centred on a district hospital. It has the District Health Team with sub-teams organised around specific activities. There is also one leader, a District Medical Officer, who is answerable to the immediate superior authority.

The district is a key conversion point where plans and policies get translated into action within the community. At the same time community needs which cannot be met locally are measured and transmitted to policy makers for future action plans. There is also a great deal of horizontal activity in the form of joint activity between sectors. As the smallest administrative unit the district has the following advantages:

1. Well-defined administrative boundaries.
2. A small and manageable bureaucracy with a few key officers who are also in frequent informal and social contact.
3. The physical distances are relatively reduced in that most parts of the district are reachable within one day's travel.

In the organisation of the national health systems in most countries the Ministries of Health increasingly recognise the importance of the district as the grass-roots of the national system. 'Let us get on with the district' was the main message at the 1986 World Health Assembly. If PHC is to be founded within the community then there is the obvious need to develop professional and managerial support as close to the periphery as possible.

The 'ideal' health district

An 'ideal' health district based on the needs of PHC could be said to be one which:
- has PHC involvement in every community throughout the district;
- has an infrastructure of health facilities which provides support and basic services for all communities in the district;
- provides secondary services for health needs of a complexity which cannot be met at a lower level;
- has considerable autonomy over its own affairs so that it can respond appropriately to local needs; has control over its own resources, and makes its own decisions;
- has effective links with other sectors and agencies and leaders to ensure a broad based approach to PHC;
- has active and dynamic leadership involved with health development throughout the district;
- has good managerial capability with effective systems, trained staff and skilled managers;
- has considerable co-ordinating capability and flexibility to ensure effective response to changing and often difficult circumstances.

In practice, there are few such 'ideal' districts, but many districts possess many of the attributes to some degree and have the potential for improvement.

The estimated workload

An estimated annual workload in a typical rural district with a population of 200 000 may be:

Deliveries at 40 per 1000 population	=	8 000
Early foetal wastage (10 per cent)	=	800
Number of pregnant women to be attended to	=	8 800
Babies with low birth weight (15 per cent)	=	1 320
Neonatal mortality	=	400
Neonatal morbidity ($\times$ 4 to 5 times)	=	1 600 to 2 000
Infant mortality (at 120 per 1000 live births)	=	1 050
Infant morbidity ($\times$ 4 to 5 times)	=	4 to 5 000
Deaths in children 1–5 years old (70/1000)	=	2 800
Morbidity rate ($\times$ 3 to 4 times)	=	8 to 9 000

The above mortality and morbidity will be distributed amongst the settlement, villages and towns scattered over the district. Primary Health Care activities, as described in Chapter 2, Fig. 2.1, operating through the existing health infrastructure will be the district's response. But that is not enough. Not every village or settlement has a sub-centre or a clinic. Even in larger villages and towns where health centres or clinics may be present they are swamped with a large workload. Hence one way of extending PHC into every settlement will be through a community based core programme focussed largely on the vulnerable groups, as shown in Fig. 5.1. Intersectoral

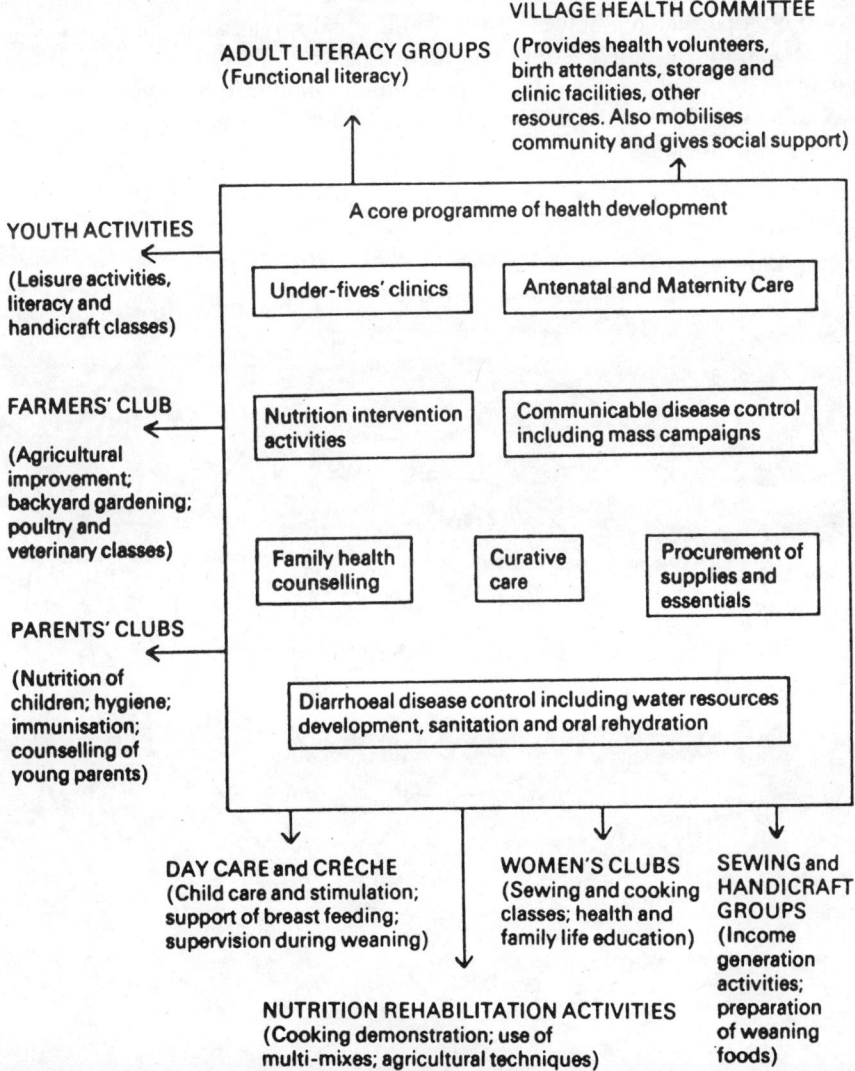

Fig. 5.1   A core health programme

collaboration operating through community groups as demonstrated in the figure will buttress the health programme and also enmesh it within the social milieu.

Linking together the widely scattered health activities will require a number of functions to be performed, for example co-ordination and supervision; training of all cadres; maintenance of records; monitoring and evaluation to name a few.

Through its health programme and other related activities the 'ideal' district will aim to achieve a number of goals in health for the individual, the family and the community. This is illustrated in Fig. 5.2. At each level there has to be a partnership between the governmental services and the beneficiary. Health cannot be handed out. The main function of PHC is to serve as an 'enabler'. It enables individuals, families and communities to find their own way to health. In the ideal district the health objectives to be sought at these three levels are described in Fig. 5.2.

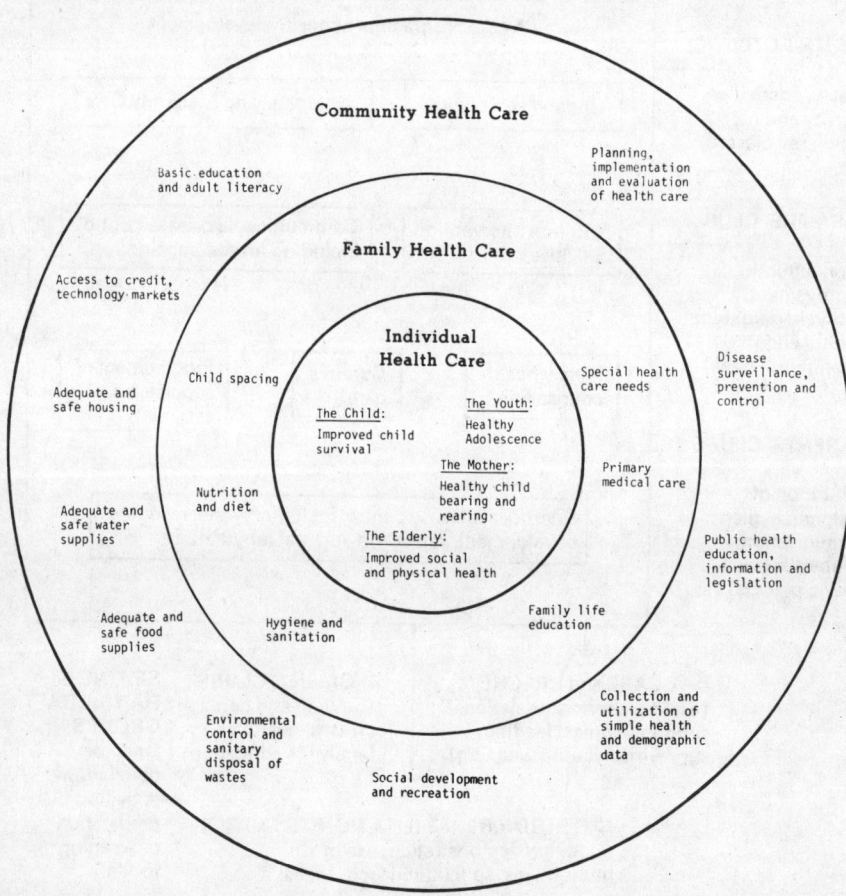

Fig. 5.2 Health care of the individual, the family and the community

66

Strengthening the capability of districts

The ideal district is a distant objective which nations may strive to achieve in a number of ways, all aiming to strengthen the capability of the district for delivering PHC. These include the following:

Decentralisation

A number of governments have plans to decentralise, but there are limits to what is always possible. Powers can never be totally devolved from the centre, especially where there are internal and external threats to the existing power structure. Decentralisation entails a different range of responsibilities and functions for both the centre and the districts, for example: new systems and procedures for financial accountability have to be developed; local autonomy can only be increased in line with an increase in local managerial capability.

There are practical reasons for delaying decentralisation in some instances. Some countries have found that the regional planning bodies are dominated by proponents of hospital services who give PHC less priority (for example Sudan and Chile). Administrative and managerial skills may not be available at the district level. Excessive decentralisation may cause waste through duplication of effort, for example in training or ordering supplies. To overcome these difficulties countries have adopted a number of different strategies for achieving decentralisation, for example:
1. Training and technical assistance for district level managers.
2. Development of national guidelines for planning and implementation.
3. Gradual devolution of responsibility guided by central monitoring and control.
4. Central funding for specific activities and programmes.

Local planning

As inputs to National Development Plans, districts are being encouraged to produce their own Five Year Development Plans and use them as a basis for shorter-term One Year Plans. In turn these are used as the basis for allocating financial resources, budgetting and local financial management. In practice, the development of the necessary planning and financial procedures can be a slow process requiring technical support and much clarification and change in existing ways of doing things to produce coherent national and local systems.

Restructuring

District organisation structures have often been developed over a number of years without guiding principles other than to meet a particular need or crisis as it arose. With the need to rationalise district infrastructure have come efforts to produce new organisation structures, for example distinguishing organisational levels such as Level A (community activities),

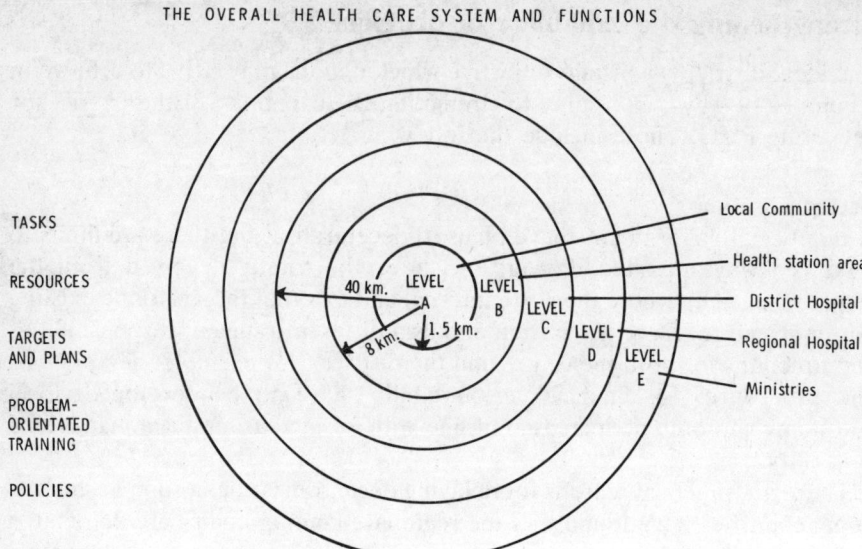

Fig. 5.3   Organisational levels for health care

Level B (health centres), Level C (district); creating PHC or Rural Health 'Units'; linking health facilities with their surrounding communities; establishing 'teams' for specific tasks and at different levels, for example MCH and EPI Teams; Health Centre Teams; District Management Teams (Fig. 5.3). Some difficult structural problems have not had such simple solutions, for example co-ordinating management arrangements for hospitals and PHC; balancing curative, preventive and managerial responsibilities (a particular problem for District Medical Officers); clarifying responsibilities and relationships between and within professional groups, for example Nursing, Medical and Environmental Health Staff; collaborative arrangements to integrate PHC into co-ordinated district development.

Training and team building
The need for District Health Workers to continue to acquire social, technical and managerial skills has been recognised by the provision of special courses, training manuals and training programmes of various kinds, often with the support of external agencies. Multi-disciplinary health worker teams have also been trained together and had the benefit of 'team building' exercises in the working situation.

Systems, and standard operating procedures
These have been developed to meet specific needs, for example drug distribution systems to ensure the reliable provision of basic drugs at peripheral levels; EPI Programmes with emphasis on the detailed requirements of the Cold Chain; new procedures concerned with systematic growth monitoring,

management information, transport scheduling, systematic PHC support, etc. The implementation of all these systems presents a major challenge to districts with limited resource and managerial capability.

Policy reviews
As other changes have been made, the existing policies have needed review. For example, personnel policies with regard to local recruitment, discipline, placement and transfer of staff; standing orders regarding local purchasing, financial controls, hospital policies in relation to PHC, all have needed to be re-thought, discussed and implemented afresh.

Reorientation to PHC

Underlying all these necessary developments in district management has been the necessity for health workers and decision-makers to reappraise their attitudes regarding the nature of appropriate health services. Only where there is understanding and commitment to the principles of PHC can other changes to strengthen district management be fully appreciated and willingly implemented. Hence various means have been used to bring about widespread reorientation towards PHC – seminars and workshops have stimulated new thinking; visits and study tours have given district workers new insights; and pilot projects have given them direct involvement in community based PHC.

In outlining these various activities the impression may be given of a great deal of activity taking place in districts. Whilst in most districts a great deal needs to be done, in some countries the criticism has been made that there has been too much activity and that district managers are unable to cope with the continual introduction of new projects and activities. There is never sufficient time for consolidation before something new is introduced. There is some truth in this criticism but it only underlines the range and complexity of changes that need to take place if there is to be effective provision and support for PHC on a wide scale.

What is impressive is that progress has been made, albeit piecemeal, in many districts, so that it is now much clearer to see a) the range of activities and changes that are needed to enable districts to provide effective support to PHC, and b) the means that can be used to help bring those changes about.

Examples can be drawn from countries where systematic efforts have been made to strengthen district health management.

Kenya is a country where over the years a national health infrastructure of basic health services has been built up with district hospitals, health centres, dispensaries and more recently community based health care in a number of pilot districts. This infrastructure is slowly being

69

extended elsewhere. Kenya has been fortunate in the extent of external aid and support it has received. Much of it has been directed to specific projects concerned with nutrition, MCH, family planning, drugs management, etc. In recent years an 'Integrated Rural Health and Family Planning Project' was designed as a means of co-ordinating external donor assistance. An important part of the project was concerned with strengthening management support, in addition to programme inputs concerned with MCH, Family Planning, PHC, essential drugs, etc. This entailed technical assistance with management training and team training for District Health Management Teams (DHMTs).

The DHMT Team Training Programme entailed bringing together a number of DHMTs (District Medical Officer, Matron, Administrator, District Clinical Officer, District Public Health Nurse, District Health Officer, District Health Education Officer) usually from the same Province at six to twelve month intervals to work in teams to develop skills of team working, problem-solving, and to be trained in the procedures of the new planning and budgetting systems. In between the workshops DHMTs returned to their districts to implement their new skills and procedures, reporting back at subsequent workshops on progress made and difficulties encountered. DHMTs identified many problems in their own districts, for which they came up with their own solutions, making use of local available resources. For example,

1. Scheduling supervisory visits to health centres and dispensaries.
2. Organising routine vehicle maintenance.
3. Improving stores procedures.
4. Developing closer links with health related sectors.
5. Extending the roles of hospital staff to support rural health units.
6. Improving financial management procedures.

In addition, a programme of district based continuing education was undertaken. DHMTs were trained to carry out an Identification of Training Needs in their own districts, and then with a minimum of external assistance, to run in-service training programmes to meet priority needs. In this way some unusual needs for staff training were identified and met, and a great deal of training skills and expert knowledge within districts was released.

Efforts put into building strong and self-confident DHMTs have paid off in other ways. In the 'pilot' PHC districts DHMT members played a major part in establishing dialogue with villages, carrying out community diagnosis and organising training for community health workers. In one district the DHMT joined forces with all other non-governmental organisations (NGOs) involved in health work in the district to produce and implement a joint health plan. In another district the DHMT planned and carried out successfully an intensive campaign against diarrhoea and vomiting.

Provincial Management Teams have provided continuing support for DHMTs. For example, at least one Provincial Team now continues to organise regular workshops for DHMT in addition to routine meetings where new policies and procedures are discussed leading to changes both in the Districts and at central policy-making levels.

A follow-up to the programme of DHMT workshops was an exercise in intensive Team Building which took place in three districts. In each the work of individual DHMT members and the team as a whole was observed throughout a six month period with the aid of staff and postgraduate students of the University of Nairobi's Departments of Community Health and Advanced Nursing. Feedback was given to individual managers and the DHMT, leading to individual Job Improvement Plans and strategies for improving performance of the DHMT and the district as a whole. In addition, feedback was given to the Ministry of Health on issues which affected district managerial performance in general. These issues included:

1. The need for planned, district programmes of community based PHC.
2. Need for central co-ordination of PHC development.
3. Need for redefinition of roles and tasks for PHC especially for District Medical Officers, Hospital Secretaries, District Clinical Officers, etc.
4. Implementation of routine management systems based on targets, reports and reviews.
5. Reviewing and strengthening organisational structures based on Rural Health Units.
6. Reviewing the functions of district hospitals in relation to PHC.
7. Establishing formal planning and collaborative links with NGOs and other sectors.
8. Reviewing personnel policies and practices affecting recruitment, transfer and stability of district level staff.
9. Action Plans to strengthen district management through decentralisation.
10. Strengthening the supportive/enabling role of Provincial Managers towards District Management Teams.
11. Strengthening the capabilities of the Ministry of Health to sustain programmes of planned organisational change.

Within the Ministry of Health, a recognition of the need to strengthen district management for effective PHC led to a decision to work intensively in three districts as part of a WHO collaborating districts programme. The aim of the programme was to strengthen district management through team-building and related management development activities. Financial support over a five year period was offered to assist the specified districts in team-building to strengthen the effectiveness of Rural Health Units; improving transport management and health information systems; and in assistance to a range of other activities which would support better planning and management in each district. District management teams were encouraged to build on their own initiatives and to devise solutions to management problems which were appropriate for their own circumstances.

In **Bombay**, a unique opportunity arose for strengthening management support for PHC in urban slum areas. The Bombay Municipal Health Department, faced with a rapidly growing population of over 8 million, responded in 1985 to the recommendations of an All India Working Group on PHC in Urban Areas by establishing 56 health posts throughout the city, each serving a population of around 50 000. A Medical Officer (MO) and Public Health Nurse (PHN) in each Health Post were to lead a team of multi-purpose and community health workers to provide comprehensive PHC in their areas. It was decided to run a series of workshops over a period of 18 months for all the newly appointed MOs and PHNs, which would equip them to initiate PHC activities in their own areas by applying skills of community diagnosis, microplanning, programme implementation and evaluation. Key officials of the Municipal Health Department participated in the workshops as it was important to integrate existing 'vertical' programmes of immunisation, family welfare, malaria control etc. into health post activities; and also to identify other opportunities for improved management. As a result of the workshops, community surveys were carried out in the catchment areas of all health posts. Each health post team produced a map of its own area, and a profile giving a breakdown of population, problems, resources and social structure. From this information, priorities were identified reflecting the priorities of the municipal corporation (for example family planning, immunisation) and those of each local community. Some aspects of action plans were achieved, for example increased immunisation coverage and improved family planning acceptances. Stronger links were forged with local communities, working relationships were strengthened in the health post teams, and there was evidence of greater understanding of a community led, PHC approach to health care.

The workshops also highlighted a number of management problems, for example the need for reality in producing action plans – over ambitious plans led to frustration when they could not be achieved. The importance of support to health post teams was stressed, for example from higher levels of management, from 'vertical' programmes, and from other technical departments. For instance, close links with water and engineering departments are essential if community aspirations for better water and sanitation are to be realised as the basis of better health. Some problems raised by health post staff like, for example, the need for closer co-ordination with water and engineering departments could only be dealt with by higher management, and this brought out the need for desirable changes in administrative structures and in the decision making processes. Some of these needs were recognised and led to an action programme by higher management for a changed management structure, improved information and logistical systems, greater involvement of community development and social workers, and closer co-ordination between municipal departments, NGOs, medical colleges etc. Thus involvement of mid-level managers (health post teams) in a dynamic learning process of regular workshops helped to bring about needed improvements not only in their own health post areas but also in the larger management system.

In recent years, **Zambia** has had to cope with massive economic problems, through a collapse of export earnings and accumulation of huge external debt. There has been a widening of the gap between rich and poor, standards of living have fallen, poverty levels especially in rural areas have increased with serious implications for general levels of health. Despite the problems, however, Zambia has been able to take some steps to adapt its health system to present-day realities. An infrastructure of district hospitals and rural health centres has been set up, covering many though not yet all parts of the country. Community health workers are working in many areas with support from their own communities and the government health system. Progress is being made towards decentralisation and more effective local decision-making. District level health managers have produced future and short-term action plans to meet the most immediate needs. Nationwide programmes for immunisation have been commenced.

Following on from an earlier programme of training workshops for District Management Teams (DMTs) a study was made in two districts of Zambia which identified major constraints in management including:
1. Shortages of transport and fuel as an impediment to PHC support.
2. Varying degrees of understanding and commitment to PHC in communities, hospitals and the health system as a whole.
3. Discontinuity in leadership of DMTs, especially in the absence of a District Medical Officer and dependence on short-term contract expatriates.
4. Variable support to different levels especially from rural health centres to community health workers.
5. Problems of co-ordination of 'vertical' and specialist programmes.
6. Lack of procedures and information for routine monitoring, review and evaluation.
Despite the constraints, attempts to strengthen management

were made through improved systems of planning, budgetting, management information, etc., which would have effect at every level of the health system.

It was against this background that a programme based on principles of 'activity-based learning' was designed (see page 78).

The programme works within a framework of regular routine workshop meetings as follows:

1. Six monthly – National Workshops for Provincial Management Teams.
2. Quarterly – Provincial Workshops for District Management Teams.
3. Monthly – District Workshop Meetings for Rural Health Centre Teams.
4. Monthly – Rural Health Centre Workshop meetings for community health workers.

The National and Provincial Workshops are used as a means of implementing the improved planning, budgetting, financial control and information systems which themselves work within an annual cycle of:

1. Producing one year forward plans and priorities.
2. Translating forward plans into estimates.
3. Reconciling estimates with financial allocations.
4. Controlling expenditure and activities within actual allocations.

The workshops are also a channel for feedback of information to and from the centre and a means of imparting skills and techniques as new programmes and activities are developed.

The District and Rural Health Centre Workshop meetings provide a routine framework for PHC support. CHWs are encouraged to visit their local health centre on the same day each month to meet with their fellow CHWs and other health workers, present reports, discuss problems, receive training and decide on activities for the forthcoming month. Similarly health centre staff meet regularly at the District Centre to present reports; receive drugs, supplies, pay, etc.; participate in training sessions and co-ordinate action-plans within the district. This regular monthly cycle provides a structure for the district information and review system and provides essential input to the DMT for its regular quarterly meeting at the provincial level.

Thus there is a routine system of communication which links different levels throughout the health system, encourages teamwork and provides a vehicle for routine monitoring, support, training and programme management at each level.

In all these examples from Kenya, India and Zambia, the importance of management teams has been stressed. But district level health managers, whether formally constituted as a District Management Team or not, need to feel a sense of responsibility and commitment to their district, and to have the freedom to plan and make decisions for its wellbeing. This to a greater or lesser extent, entails decentralisation. Even though countries are moving in the direction of decentralisation, total decentralisation is unlikely. In many countries the realities of power politics require that there be strong central authority and control. This may be necessary to maintain a strong sense of national unity, but also to ensure equity in allocation of resources between different parts of the country, and to ensure commitment to national goals and priorities. This is particularly important where a country has expressed a clear commitment to PHC, backed up by appropriate strategies and allocation of resources.

The question therefore is not whether to decentralise or not, but how to develop a system for PHC management which has the advantages of both, and where there are effective linkages between central and local levels. Similar issues of decentralisation apply within the district itself, for one of the key principles of PHC is that the powers of individuals and communities over their own health matters is increased. This entails greater autonomy for communities, and for 'first-level' facilities (health centres etc.) which give immediate support to communities.

The 'process' of achieving greater decentralisation also requires careful and sensitive handling. Autonomous health districts, planning and deciding for themselves, call for a high degree of managerial skill. Managers can only acquire such skills, however, where they have freedom to decide and manage their own situations. This therefore calls for programmes to decentralise and for strengthening district capability which go hand in hand with efforts to develop the necessary managerial skills.

Changes needed to strengthen district level management

A large catalogue can be made of aspects of management that need to be strengthened at district level to enable effective support to be given to PHC. These include:

1. Managerial leadership, understanding and commitment to PHC principles
The practice and support for PHC is a complex subject with many facets. Most district health organisations have been based on a curative model, so it is essential that district managers have an understanding and commitment to PHC if they are to make the necessary changes. The ideal is to have as leader a District Medical Officer with a public health background who has effective control over both hospital and community services. There is a dearth of such people, and many more need to be trained. In the absence of such appropriately trained individuals the leadership of District Health Teams presents real problems. Frequently leadership will fall to a hospital doctor without time, skills or interest in PHC, with the result that resources and services continue to be skewed heavily towards curative care. An alternative

solution is for PHC leadership to go to a senior nurse, health inspector or specially designated PHC co-ordinator. This can work provided they have strong medical backing, not least in ensuring adequate resources for PHC support.

Managers of District Health Teams will have to address the following issues:

2. A continuous programme for extension and maintenance of PHC   Health For All by the Year 2000 requires that there be essential health care in every village and community. There are, as yet, very few districts in which this has been achieved.

3. Teamwork   There needs to be an effective District Management Team for planning, co-ordination and monitoring of district services, but in addition there need to be teams for particular programmes (for example, immunisation), and to ensure co-operation between departments and agencies.

4. Hospital control and management   Secondary services need to be well run, but not at the expense of PHC, and active programmes for hospital involvement in PHC are needed.

5. Planning   Each district needs a long-term forward plan, based on health needs and problems, but also short-term annual operational plans and monthly detailed action plans.

6. Financial control   This entails preparing annual estimates and budgets, revising them in the light of funds available, and controlling the spending of money. In practice, the financial management function in districts is very poorly developed.

7. Controlling resources   especially of time, personnel, supplies and transport. Resources are limited, but much can be made of little with good management.

8. Systems and procedures   are needed for particular programmes but also for the logistics of such things as drugs and supplies distribution, scheduling of visits, training, monitoring and evaluation. A particular need is to have co-ordinated systems which will continue to work in difficult circumstances.

It is because of the scale and complexity of these changes that continuing activity is needed to strengthen district management. In a number of countries this need has been recognised, and strengthening of district management has become an important feature of health development programmes. Producing such changes is a complex task, and results of change are likely to be seen over a period of time rather than immediately. Some common features of such change strategies can, however, be identified as follows:

1. Defining districts geographically in terms of catchment areas, but also in relation to administrative boundaries, registration districts etc.

2. Training This is most effective when directed to the specific needs of district managers. In India, the National Institute of Health and Family Welfare has carried out a major study to define roles and tasks of managers at each level (for example District and Block Medical Officers), as a basis for detailed training programmes. Elsewhere, team training for members of existing management teams is increasingly being used, and there is a growing emphasis on leadership training for those in key positions.

3. Clarification of roles and responsibilities This is particularly important where there has been a rapid growth of PHC programmes and there is overlapping or confusion about managerial responsibilities. In some places, new roles are being created, for example in Zimbabwe of a District Health Services Administrator. In other places existing roles are being strengthened, for example nurse managers in Botswana who take responsibility for PHC in the absence of medical officers.

4. Increasing financial responsibilities of district management This is usually as part of improved systems of budgetting and financial control, and calls for staff with accountancy and financial management skills at district level. In some countries, emphasis is being given to local fund-raising, which increases the spending freedom of the local management.

5. Increased authority is also being given to local management in some countries in matters concerned with recruitment, selection, discipline of staff, etc. Where local decision-making is encouraged, there is frequently an increase in local management's problem-solving capability, and capacity for flexible 'adaptive' styles of management.

6. Bottom-up planning This is essential if local needs are to be reflected in long-term strategic plans, and is facilitated where there are such mechanisms as District Planning Councils, and co-ordinated planning systems.

7. Systems development This may require detailed operational research and concerted efforts to improve existing systems, but much is being achieved in many places in systems concerned with information, transport scheduling and maintenance, revolving drug funds etc. Management guides and manuals are also of help in improving routine working procedures.

8. Increasing community control of health services In some countries local health authorities give local representatives a greater say in health management. Elsewhere this is achieved through strengthening links with local government, district development committees etc.

9. Donor aid   There is an increasing tendency for aid for specific projects (for example family planning, immunisation) to be given to individual districts. In Kenya, technical assistance is being provided to pilot districts to improve their managerial capabilities; in Bangladesh and Zimbabwe similar assistance is given to a number of districts as part of a comprehensive programme of strengthening health services' delivery systems.

10. District hospitals   Their role is crucial to effective PHC management, which can be helped by a systematic effort to clarify and redefine the function of each hospital department in relation to PHC.

11. Incentives for district level workers   Policies are needed which encourage workers to stay in districts long enough to make an effective contribution. This may entail the provision of housing, educational facilities, improved pay and conditions of service, long service awards etc.

12. Health management resource centres   have been set up in the West Indies, to disseminate ideas on improved health management. In Kenya, a basic library, including management texts, has been provided for each district.

13. Integration of 'vertical' programmes   Strong vertical programmes, for example for malaria control and immunisation are a feature in many countries, and are effective in promoting individual programmes, but in the long run can work against the establishment of comprehensive and strong district management.

In some countries successful efforts have been made to integrate certain activities through planned programmes, with a greater emphasis on response to particular district needs and priorities.

In conclusion, it may be said that much of the effort to manage change for improved PHC needs to be focussed at the district level. This will entail helping district managers to develop skills for managing change; giving them freedom and encouragement to initiate needed changes; and allocating resources direct to districts to facilitate change.

Appendix: Principles of activity based learning

Activity based learning is an approach to training which takes place largely within the working environment. It has many advantages when used to assist managers to develop and run an effective PHC support system.
These advantages include:
1. Learning is part of the normal working situation − it takes place largely in working time, within the management situation, and using managers as both trainers and learners.
2. Learning is a continuous process − managers are continually learning

new skills and approaches and putting them into practice.

3. Learning is a 2-way process – managers learn about the needs and problems of their own organisations and communities, and share skills and knowledge with fellow workers on how to tackle those problems.

4. Theory is immediately put into practice. Because training is related to immediate problems, theory must be relevant. In addition, new ideas can immediately be tested and applied to the local situation. Thus, feedback is built into the learning situation, so that errors can be eliminated, and successes reinforced.

5. Learning is part of a co-ordinated system of:
   a) Micro-planning – planning skills are learnt as plans are prepared, and implementation skills are learnt as plans are put into action.
   b) Support and supervision – designated supervisors and those they supervise share membership of action based learning groups and learn together how to solve problems and improve performance.
   c) Team-building – through group learning, teams (for example District Management Teams, Rural Health Centre Teams) who work together, learn together how to achieve common goals.
   d) Information and evaluation – training is based on information on problems in the district, and is therefore evaluated in terms of its effects in reducing those problems.
   e) Communications – continuous learning requires the strengthening of communications systems between managers, health workers, community members and different levels of the health system.
   f) Payment, supplies and transport systems – use is made of existing systems, for example training takes place on days when pay is collected, drugs distributed etc.

6. Co-operation is encouraged through regular meetings of managers and workers.

7. There is built in monitoring, in that effects of training on working practice are reviewed at subsequent training sessions, and necessary action taken.

8. Motivation of managers and workers is increased as they become more confident and see the results of training in their work, thereby avoiding the frustration of learning new things without being able to apply them.

9. Organisational infrastructure is strengthened. This is done by ensuring regular contact between provincial, district, health centre and community workers.

10. Managerial responsibility and accountability is strengthened – managers are responsible for training those who are accountable to them.

11. Low cost. As existing facilities are used, there are few additional costs, for example for hotel accommodation etc.

12. Learning is consistent with a 'community supportive' approach to PHC. It encourages an open flow of communication and response to community needs.

Further reading

Amonoo-Lartson, R., Ebrahim, G.J., Lovel, H.J. and Ranken, J.P., *District health care, Challenges for planning, organisation and evaluation in developing countries*, London, Macmillan Press Ltd, 1984.

Kleczkowski, B.M., Elling, R.H., Smith, D.L., *Health System Support for Primary Health Care*, Geneva, World Health Organisation, 1984.

McMahon, R., Barton, E., Piot, M., *On being in charge: A guide for middle-level management in Primary Health Care*, Geneva, World Health Organisation, 1980.

World Health Organisation, *Intermediate level support for Primary Health Care, a framework for analysis and action*, Offset Publication SHS/82.2, Geneva, WHO 1982.

World Health Organisation, *Managerial process for national health development*, Health for All Series No. 5, Geneva, WHO, 1981.

CHAPTER 6
Hospitals and Primary Health Care

'Hospitals cannot be isolated from Primary Health Care.... They are too powerful to be ignored. Many have knowledge and a functional capacity that must be tapped by Primary Health Care. They shape the public and professional image of health in a manner which must be radically altered if the health for all movement is to obtain universal support.'

Dr. H. Mahler, Director General of the WHO

Many of the spectacular developments in medical science have led to an undue dependence on medical technology for curing diseases rather than identifying their cause for prevention. A great deal of the new technology has come to be enshrined in hospitals. The focus of curative care in hospitals has tended to gradually slide from care of acute illness to intensive care. This has resulted in undue professional dominance by the hospital consultant on the one hand and a mystification of medicine on the other. Market forces have resulted in high pressure salesmanship for much of the new medical technology. Unnecessary hospitalisation, excessive or unwarranted use of drugs (for example, corticosteroids and antibiotics), vitamins and baby foods; excessive use of laboratory investigations and unnecessary surgical procedures (for example Caesarian sections) are some of the examples. Increasing costs and sophistication of medical practice have tended to increase the difficulties of the lowest social classes in having access to medical institutions. Thus, the hospital has come to be an instrument of social domination and economic exploitation instead of part of the national system of improving health. With characteristic foresight Mahatma Gandhi had warned that 'A multiplicity of hospitals is not a test of civilisation. It is rather a symptom of decay.'

PHC has come to be looked upon as a challenge to professional status rather than an opportunity for improving the health of the masses. This is understandable. Almost the entire professional training takes place in hospitals. Hence that is the environment in which the health professional is conditioned to function. The textbooks used during training have diseases and etiology, pathology, symptomatology and case management as their focus. The skills needed for working in the community like, for example, social, political, managerial skills as well as those of communication are hardly ever taught during professional training. Moreover, the social and professional prestige, together with the adulation of the large number of the sick who throng hospitals create a climate in which the professional fails to see beyond the boundaries of the hospital.

Three commitments demanded by PHC

The philosophy of PHC and the background of events leading to its development have been discussed in Chapter 2. For the hospitals the significant commitments asked for are three:

1. *Health care must extend to ALL,* regardless of physical, social or cultural distance. Whereas the tradition in hospital reports is to report on numbers served, for example outpatient attendance; bed occupancy; surgical procedures carried out; deliveries conducted and so on, PHC concentrates on the *unreached.* Those who do not or cannot make regular use of services for financial, social or cultural reasons or because of distance are of greater interest than those who do.
2. *The focus must be on the common health problems of the community,* and the most cost-effective way of dealing with them. The hospital tradition is to discuss the rare and 'interesting' problems in clinical meetings, but PHC concentrates on what is afflicting the majority of the population and how the situation can be improved.
3. *Hospitals traditionally create dependency* The patient is removed from family and home for close observation, intensive care, laboratory investigation and monitoring response to treatment. All these mystify medical care. PHC concentrates on enabling individuals, families and communities to care for themselves. Hence the need for simplification; for appropriate technology; and for creation of health awareness. In the pursuit of scientific excellence it is helpful to bear in mind that the most useful scientific innovations are those which simplify health measures so that they can be performed by lesser trained people.

Changing the relationship between the hospital and the community

The above three commitments demanded by PHC require a change in the relationship between the hospital and the community in which it is located. There will have to be a basic change in the culture of the hospital and this calls for a number of fundamental changes as described in Table 6.1.

It is obvious that the task is going to be uphill. There are too many powerful forces including hospital administrators, specialists and the elite groups who need to be converted. The commitment to PHC must be unconditional, unambiguous and unwavering. It stands to reason that if over 90

Table 6.1 Changes needed for hospitals to become more responsive to PHC

	Present	→	Change of emphasis	→	PHC supportive
WHO ARE SERVED?	Mostly those within the city boundary and within five mile radius	→	Wider coverage	→	Not only those who attend but also those who do not or cannot
WHAT IS THE MAIN CONCERN OF THE SERVICE?	High quality care for complicated rare illnesses	→	Identification of those at risk in the context of wide coverage	→	Preventive care for all; early diagnosis to prevent advanced disease
WHAT IS THE MAIN FOCUS?	Recent advances in biotechnology	→	Creation of health awareness	→	Simplification of medical knowledge and use of appropriate technology
WHO ARE THE DECISION MAKERS?	Senior consultants	→	Democratisation of decision making	→	Jointly with community representatives
WHAT DETERMINES THE LONG TERM GOALS?	International trends; new technology; market forces	→	Real needs	→	Social epidemiology

per cent of deaths fall into just four preventable categories — malnutrition, infectious illnesses, diarrhoeal disease and respiratory infection — then putting resources into intensive care is the least profitable way of dealing with them.

Several countries have evolved imaginative approaches for linking hospitals with PHC.

In **Costa Rica** during the past 25 years a programme called 'Hospitals without Walls' has been evolved. In this programme each area hospital is linked with four health centres and 45 health posts within the area of 1.35 sq km, with 86 000 inhabitants. All these three levels of care operate as one functional entity within the organised community. There is a regular two-way flow vertically between the various levels of health care, and also horizontally at each level with the community. Elected representatives of the people at each level serve as links with the community. A great deal of environmental improvement has been achieved including safe water; sanitation; higher standard of living and better nutrition. Goals which at one time seemed impossible have been reached through popular participation. Rural roads, aqueducts, health posts and regional buildings have been constructed through self-help. Several deficiencies in medical and nursing training have been corrected through curriculum change, and a number of standard medical practices have been modified. Since 1971 when the programme of 'Hospitals without Walls' started there has been marked improvement in health indices. Infant mortality has come down from 60 to 16 per 1000; mortality in the age group 1 to 4 years has fallen from 2 to 0 46 per 1000. Hospital deliveries have risen from 75 per cent to 98 per cent of all births.

Other countries have achieved similar results through different routes.

In **China**, prior to the Cultural Revolution of the sixties, the work of the orthodox medical professions was largely focussed on urban areas where only 20 per cent of the population lived. The Cultural Revolution attacked the privileges of the medical establishment and not less than one third of health professionals were ordered to the countryside. A rapid and subtle development of rural services began to happen as the medical establishment recognised that it could not cope unaided with the mass of work in the countryside. Neither could it expect to return to the work and comparative comfort of the towns without leaving an effective system in place. This gave a tremendous impetus to the development of 'barefoot doctors' or health auxiliaries.

In **India**, every medical school has been made responsible for total health care of one administrative block which may be used also as a training area for the medical and nursing students. The Christian

---

Medical College in Vellore has taken this opportunity to extend the activities of its Rural Unit for Health and Social Affairs (RUHSA) which had been established since 1977. RUHSA has been involved in a rural health and development programme in a block (an administrative unit in India) of about 100 000 inhabitants, living in 83 villages and hamlets. A survey at the commencement of RUHSA's activities had shown that more than three quarters of the population lived below the poverty line. The objectives of RUHSA's programme have been the following:

1. In the health sector
— To increase accessibility to health services by setting up health facilities and training local personnel to create a pattern of services consistent with local resources.
— To improve the quality of prenatal and maternity care, and the coverage with immunisation.

2. In the economic sector
— To improve the economic status of families living below the poverty line through training and credit facilities for new enterprise.
— To develop programmes oriented towards creating local employment.

3. In the social sector
— To establish and revitalise women's clubs, nursery schools and youth organisations.
— To establish village advisory committees to help with the running of the peripheral health facilities.

4. In the education sector
— To improve adult literacy through evening classes.
— To achieve a general raising of awareness, co-operation and participation from individuals and the community.
   Several evaluation studies have shown remarkable achievements in health and general welfare of the population served.

These case studies illustrate the ways in which hospitals can become the pivots for PHC activities in the communities they serve.

Three core functions for hospitals in support of PHC

In an international conference on 'The Role of Hospitals in Primary Health Care', sponsored by the World Health Organisation and the Aga Khan Foundation in 1981, a number of core functions for hospitals were identified. This conference was a follow-on to the process started at Alma-Ata in 1978. The three core functions identified were the following:

1. Direct support for PHC

Firstly, in most countries, hospitals serve as a focal point for referral, but in a disorganised and impersonal manner. There is little professional contact on a regular basis between the hospital specialists and the peripheral workers. Hence self-referral by patients is more common than through the official channels. Often the process deteriorates into the 'by-pass' phenomenon, so that patients go directly to the hospital avoiding their local health centre. This creates low morale and self-esteem amongst the front-line workers. At the same time it results in expensive secondary and tertiary care facilities being swamped with primary health care problems. Hence the referral system needs to be better organised.

Secondly, hospitals can support front-line workers through continuing education; guidance and advice on problems; technical back-up and logistical support. In addition there should be mutual support for following up patients and for monitoring of various health activities.

Thirdly, hospitals can provide managerial support for the planning and organisation of the health system in their catchment areas.

2. Programmes for community health development

Hospitals can become the source of information concerning the health problems of the community. Promotive activities like the under-fives and ante-natal clinics are usually also the focal points for the dissemination of health information. Nutrition rehabilitation centres achieve the same purpose with regard to establishing healthy patterns of child nutrition. However, besides health education there is a need for dissemination of the kind of data needed for creating community awareness about health problems. Information concerning, for example, which age groups are in most need of services? What types of services? What is the utilisation rate? How effective have the services been? Which groups are not reached by the services? Coverage rates? etc. provides the raw material for decision making.

In addition to providing information about health matters of major relevance, hospitals need to be concerned with developing methods and appropriate technologies for solving health problems. The example of sugar-salt solution for oral rehydration is a good one. Based on sound scientific principles the promotion of this new technology helped the treatment for dehydration move out of the hospitals to the sub-centre level. A low-cost double-ended spoon for measuring sugar and salt in the right proportions for making one glass of the solution (instead of a sachet for one litre) helped to move the treatment of dehydration out of the sub-centre into the home. The use of rice powder instead of sugar made the treatment available to an even larger number of families. Thus, with every step the treatment for dehydration became available to an ever increasing number of families. Its social marketing on a global scale by UNICEF has already produced an estimated saving of 1.5 million lives in 1987.

A second example of appropriate technology is that provided by the new approaches in the management of tuberculosis. Treatment of patients in sanatoria until full recovery was not only expensive but also meant an inevitable loss of income for their families. Only the better-off could benefit from the treatment. When epidemiologic research showed that all that mattered was the correct use of chemotherapy, the treatment of tuberculosis was revolutionised. The poor could now be treated as out-patients. When it was discovered that alternative day treatment given as one morning dose was as effective as dosing three times daily, the management of tuberculosis moved out of the hospitals into the community. Now a team of district nurses could visit the patient at home on alternate days to give an injection of streptomycin and supervise the swallowing of the tablets of isoniazid/thiacetozane. But the greatest advantage was that now the patient could continue working after an initial period of three to four weeks of intensive therapy to sterilise the sputum. Such innovative approaches for all common conditions are urgently needed.

– In all countries there is a need to combat false health information. The infant food industry, the tobacco industry, the brewing industry and the pharmaceutical industry have all caused international concern because of their promotional practices. Because of their prestige in the community the hospitals are best placed to combat false information, and can generate the head of political pressure for putting a curb on such practices.

– The district and regional level hospitals are also close to the administrative machinery. Contacts with other services like agriculture, education, water and sanitation and so on are easy. Hence hospitals are well placed for initiating the organisational structures and processes for intersectoral collaboration. By setting up collaborative programmes in the communities immediately around them, the various services can learn from experience about the problems to be encountered.

– As decentralisation becomes a common practice district and regional hospitals will find themselves closely linked to local political bodies, as in Tanzania (Chapter 2, page 17). Hospitals may then be able to play a greater role in encouraging decision-making within the community, so that communities can have a control over their own health. In order to help communities make rational choices it would be necessary to provide them with information of an epidemiological and behavioural nature. Hence the need for hospitals to study community dynamics in addition to health problems.

3. Basic and continuing education of health personnel
Front-line hospitals are in a unique position to analyse community health situations as well as to help individuals and community groups to do so. They can thus draw upon real-life experiences for health development activities, and enlarge their role beyond that of curative care into promotive and preventive work as well as rehabilitation.

The training activities of the hospitals can extend beyond the confines of the classroom into the communities. Regular workshops in which hospital staff and workers from peripheral units exchange experiences out of which health strategies are evolved will be one way of addressing local health problems. Such educational activities will help to involve the hospital with the rest of the health infrastructure and at the same time sharpen the skills and knowledge of front-line workers.

People's councils at all tiers of the health services (Levels A, B and C of Fig. 6.1, page 90) may be invited to participate in workshops and to influence policy, management and resources. Existing programmes may be evaluated in such workshops and new targets set in the light of past experiences.

Processes of hospital involvement in PHC

The three main areas of involvement identified at the Karachi conference viz. direct support of PHC, community health development activities and basic and continuing education of health personnel outline the main processes through which hospitals can become the springboard of PHC within their catchment area. These processes are best summarised by the acronym HOSPITAL:

Aim	*Processes*
Support of PHC	Health services in catchment area
	Operational research
	Supervisory support for levels 1° (A) and 2° (B)
Community health development activities	Planning
	Information generation and dissemination
Basic and continuing education of health personnel	Training and continuing education incorporating the eight elements of PHC
	Augmenting referral system through regular contact
	Logistic support

If these processes are to get firmly rooted and flourish hospitals will have to change their culture. Instead of being the receiving station of 'interesting cases' referred by the peripheral clinics the emphasis will now be on an outgoing flow of information, technical support, materials and equipment to strengthen the front-line. Coverage has to have priority over diagnosis of rare diseases; better nutrition through local food production over treatment of deficiency disorders; intersectoral activities over isolated excellence. Such a change of emphasis requires a great deal of reorientation. That such a reorientation is possible is demonstrated by the examples from several countries described at the beginning of the chapter. With the current ethos in the profession it is, however, likely to be an uphill task unless medical and nursing education is reorganised (see Chapters 7 and 8).

When hospitals have been established with the specific purpose of health development in their catchment populations reorientation has not been difficult.

In **Bangladesh**, the Gonoshasthaya Kendra — The People's Health Centre — grew from the vision of a team of doctors and medical students during the liberation struggle of 1971. Out of a small 15-bed hospital arose a complex programme of rural upliftment with PHC as the main focus, but also including agriculture extension, skills training, and local production of essential drugs. The health programme is largely based on medical auxiliaries, some of whom have been trained even in surgery. An agricultural extension programme helps the landless with deriving income from new sources and the small farmers to maximise production. A centre for women provides vocational training in handicraft, sewing and small industry. The literacy programme has promoted adult literacy and primary education for children from disadvantaged families. A monthly newsletter provides up-to-date medical and scientific information and covers a range of political and social issues. A pharmaceutical enterprise produces essential drugs of sellable quality. A satellite programme with similar activities has been set up 180 km outside the capital, Dacca.

In general, non-governmental hospitals have found it easier to embrace PHC, and extend their activities into the catchment area. The ethos and the general philosophy of the parent organisation are a powerful influence. Many of them being Church-related, providing services to the needy rather than personal aggrandisement, is the main driving force. Secondly, they are not encumbered by a rigid bureaucracy with, at times, out-of-date regulations. Thirdly, there is no rapid turnover of staff, so that individuals have time to become committed to on-going programmes and even develop new ones. Moreover, having made a voluntary and informed decision to join the service, the staff are highly motivated. Thus, what is often lumped under 'charisma' is due to a number of analysable factors.

Putting the structures together

A core health programme has been described in Chapter 5 (page 65, Fig. 5.1). Such a programme incorporating PHC activities, collaboration between sectors, and community participation should ideally be operating at every village or settlement and urban neighbourhood in the catchment area of the hospital. The emerging structure may be conceptualised as shown in Fig. 6.1 overleaf.

At level A, the core health programme described in Fig. 6.1 is the main target of health development, with regular technical and logistical support from the hospital and on a day-to-day basis from the local sub-centre. At

Administration	Services	Expected Number of Core Programmes in a District of 200 000 Population

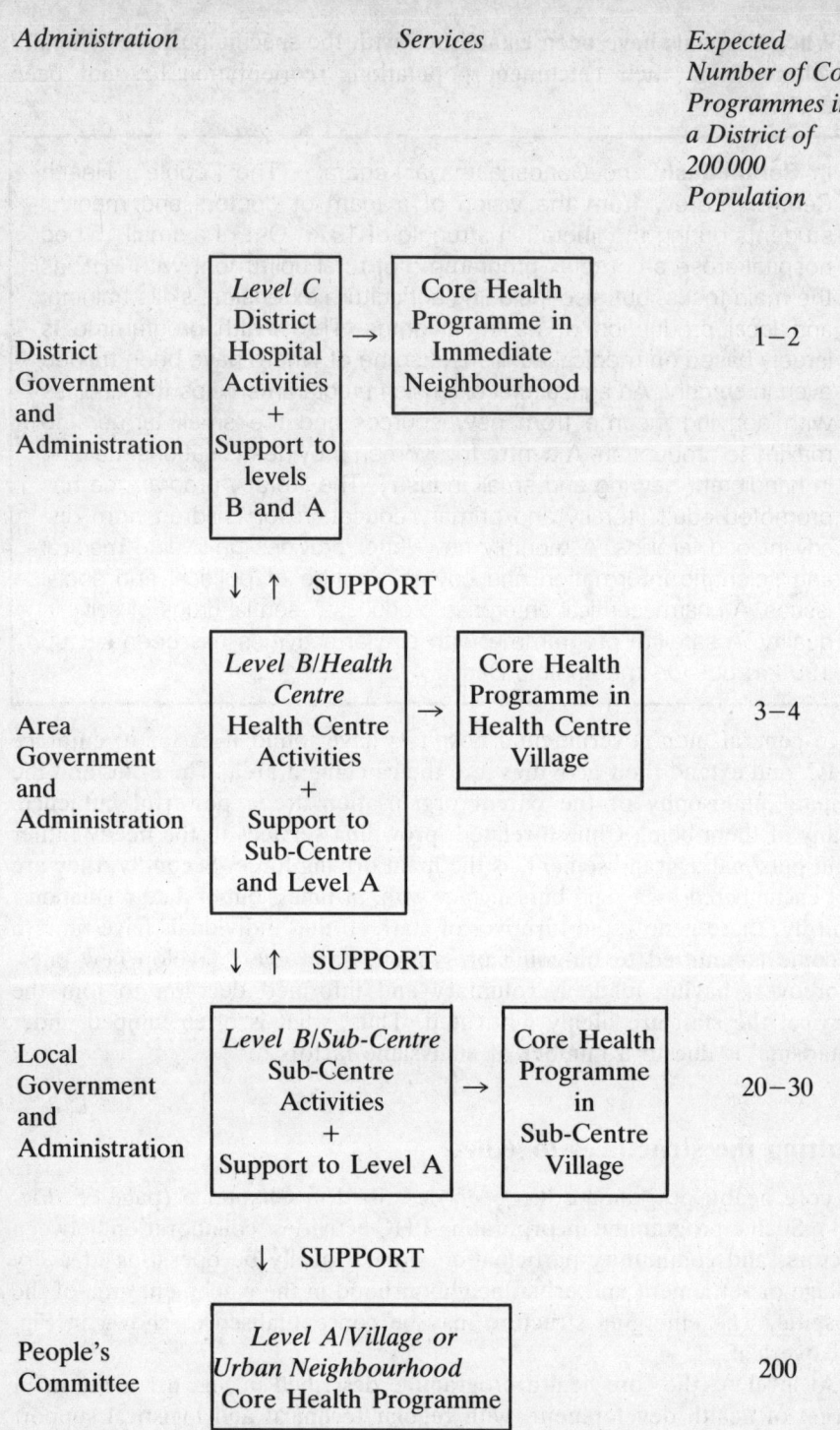

District Government and Administration	Level C District Hospital Activities + Support to levels B and A →	Core Health Programme in Immediate Neighbourhood	1–2

↓ ↑ SUPPORT

Area Government and Administration	Level B/Health Centre Health Centre Activities + Support to Sub-Centre and Level A →	Core Health Programme in Health Centre Village	3–4

↓ ↑ SUPPORT

Local Government and Administration	Level B/Sub-Centre Sub-Centre Activities + Support to Level A →	Core Health Programme in Sub-Centre Village	20–30

↓ SUPPORT

People's Committee	Level A/Village or Urban Neighbourhood Core Health Programme	200

Fig. 6.1 The hospital in district health development

level B a similar core health programme operates within the community in which the sub-centre or the health centre is situated, with support from the hospital. At each level the organised community and local government are encouraged to provide caretaker committees. Because of the reputation and prestige of the hospital, the liaison with the district's administrative machinery is best handled by the hospital administration. For the same reason the health service is best suited to be the lead agency in convening a technical committee consisting of the District Agricultural Officer, the Education Officer, the Veterinary Officer, the Water and Sanitation Engineer and so on for intersectoral activities. The responsibility for organising such an administrative structure will have to be shouldered by a department within the district health administration. The Karachi conference recommended the setting up of a department of community medicine at the hospital. However desirable, this would be a utopian dream for most poor nations except at the larger hospitals. A more practical approach will be the establishment of a new post at all district hospitals of a District Medical Officer (Rural). Together with the district maternal and child health officer, the health education officer, the public health nurse and any other similar colleague the DMO (Rural) can head a team for organising the necessary set-up for PHC. Such a team can then take on the task of integrating the hospital with PHC activities in the immediate neighbourhood as well as in the district.

Such district health teams are currently being established in **Tanzania**. After a pilot project in PHC in one of the districts of the country (page 148.) several lessons were learnt for establishing PHC nationwide. Amongst these the most important was the need for a mobile district level team for planning, administration and the day-to-day management of health activities. The district health team is to provide continuing education for peripheral workers, develop training programmes for community health workers, the traditional birth attendants and primary school teachers. The team is required to establish a dialogue with community organisations at various levels. During the monthly rounds the team is to help establish the newly trained cadres in their posts, negotiate remuneration and assist with administrative, technical or logistical problems.

Progressing towards national PHC

Country experiences like those of Tanzania help to identify the steps in the progression of the national health service towards PHC. Several functions of the front line hospitals can be lumped together as modules. Then depending upon circumstances and opportunity various modules may be put together to achieve the planned target (see Fig. 6.2 overleaf).

E = Support of front line workers. Links with community organisations	D = Special outpatients TB/Leprosy/ Sexually Transmitted Diseases/Others	C = Social module Nutrition rehabilitation/ Parents' clubs/ Health education
F = Teaching Data gathering Planning	A = Basic module Inpatients/ Maternity Outpatients/ Casualty	B = MCH module Antenatal and under-fives care/ School health

Fig. 6.2   Hospital activity modules

Currently module A is the 'basic' function of most front line hospitals. Some are able to add modules B and D to their work. The progression to adding module C can be achieved with a few additional facilities. Depending upon distances involved and facilities of transport a mobile team is needed to be responsible for modules E and F. When several additional modules have been joined to the 'basic module' it is reasonable to have a caretaker team assigned to supervise the additional activities. At that stage the Tanzanian approach would appear to be the best suited when resources are minimal.

Questions which need addressing

The foregoing discussion on structures and processes through which hospitals can become supportive of PHC raises several issues. The shift to community orientation cuts across the established interests of most professionals for specialisation and the pursuit of excellence. Hence the knowledge, skills and attitudes imparted in the formative years of training become a special issue.

In the examples of countries cited it is obvious that each nation evolves a specific pattern of health development consistent with its own traditions, circumstances and aspirations. There is no universal model. In successful national programmes health activities occur within the context of planned national development. The long-term objectives of such plans as in China, Cuba, Costa Rica, Sri Lanka and Tanzania include the establishment of people and communities to be self-reliant in health. The socio-cultural context in which health activities occur has been given prominence in all successful programmes. Communities are helped to identify their health needs and to devise ways of obtaining them. These issues help to prepare the groundwork on which PHC can flourish.

Not only do nations differ in their culture and politics so as to encourage or inhibit changes in favour of PHC, they also differ in their internal priorities and values. Within the hospital different professionals, managers and their associates place different values on their hospital's community responsibility in comparison to its other priorities. Changing a hospital's way of thinking is at least as difficult and risky as changing a community's way of thinking about health matters. Similar insights to 'community development' are required in the hospital in relation to its 'organisation development' (see Table 6.2).

Table 6.2 Comparison between community development and the development of organisations

Community development	Organisation development
Works with communities at their own level	Works within the 'culture' of the hospital
Starts and works through the community's concerns	Starts and works through issues as seen by managers and workers
Recognises the individual complexity of each community	Recognises the complexities of organisational life
Helps communities develop a sense of purpose and direction	Clarifies organisational goals and objectives
All embracing—health, families, food, power structures etc.	All embracing—work problems, systems, strategies, relationships
Releases community energies to tackle problems	Motivates employees to solve their problems
A learning process	Encourages organisational learning
Works towards self-sustaining communities	Encourages autonomous, self-reliant units and departments
Dangers of conflicts with powerful interest groups	Risks especially in bureaucratic/rigid organisations
Assisted by internal and external facilitators	Assisted by internal and external change agents

Professional and management leadership in favour of change are needed within the hospital as much as within the community.

At a practical level hospitals can find a role for themselves in the national strategy for PHC by addressing a few questions:
1. Does the hospital view its responsibilities as extending to the total catchment population? If so, what activities may be undertaken for improving the health of that population?

2. As an institution responsible for the health of the catchment population what relationships are being developed with the health providers in the area? This would include peripheral health workers in the health centres, sub-centres and health posts. It would also include traditional health providers like the traditional birth attendants.
3. If a great deal of health arises from non-health sectors, what working relationships have been established by the hospital with officials from other sectors and with community representatives?
4. Does the hospital consider it to be within its responsibility to strengthen the front line through training, ensuring regular supplies of drugs and materials, and technical support?
5. Does the hospital participate in defining the common health problems of the catchment area, the population groups commonly affected, and their distribution? Similarly, are the weak links within the health system of the area being identified and rectified?
6. Does each hospital department review its role in relation to PHC? For example, obstetrics – developing 'at risk' pregnancy programmes; surgery – ensuring high quality minor surgery in health centres; catering department – nutrition education in the hospital and further afield?
7. Does the hospital leadership continually strive to reconcile its values in respect of institutional based health care with that in the community?

When some of these questions are discussed in regular workshops by those working in hospitals, a process of change in the insular character of hospitals can begin. It is through involvement with the health problems of the entire catchment area that action learning can occur, enabling hospitals to take a lead role in the development of PHC.

Further reading

Dean, M. (Ed), *The role of hospitals in Primary Health Care*, Geneva, World Health Organisation and Aga Khan Foundation, 1982.

Ebrahim, G. J., *Paediatric Practice in Developing Countries*, London, Macmillan, 1981.

Huss, C., *A study of planned organisational change in the structure and functioning of Indian Hospitals*, New Delhi, Voluntary Health Association of India, 1975.

Macagba, R., *Hospitals and Primary Health Care*, London, International Hospital Federation, 1984.

Monekosso, G., *The role of first-line hospitals within the local health services system*, Geneva, WHO, 1980, (Mimeo.Paper SHS/SPM/ 80.2).

CHAPTER 7
Medical Education for Primary Health Care

'There is nothing more difficult to carry out, nor more doubtful of success nor more dangerous to handle than to initiate a new order of things.'

Machiavelli in 'The Prince'

The Declaration of Alma-Ata (1978) signalled the start of a 'new order of things' in health care delivery and in the training of health workers. Primary Health Care (PHC) emphasises equitable distribution of services and thus requires the development of new cadres of front line health workers, for example community health aides and volunteer village health workers responsible for bringing health care to the social and geographical periphery. The training programmes for these new kinds of health personnel have attracted considerable attention. However, this has tended to obscure the fact that a 'new order of things' is also required in the education of doctors. In spite of the current emphasis on community (village) health workers (CHW), the doctor has a key role within the PHC team and even a greatly expanded one. For what functions and tasks in PHC should medical education prepare the doctor? The doctor within the PHC team is responsible for the following:

1. Surveying the health situation of the community in order to make a diagnosis of health and other needs and problems as well as evaluating the resources available.
2. Developing a health plan for the community, emphasising equitable distribution of services.
3. Organising the provision of curative, preventive and promotive health services for the community. A small proportion of more complex curative cases will be referred to the doctor leaving him free for the more important organisational aspect of his work. Lesser trained members of the health team will manage the great majority of curative cases.
4. Managing and evaluating services, with particular emphasis on supervision of staff and monitoring of on-going provision of care.
5. Continuing education for members of the PHC team.

1. The 'Curative Chair'

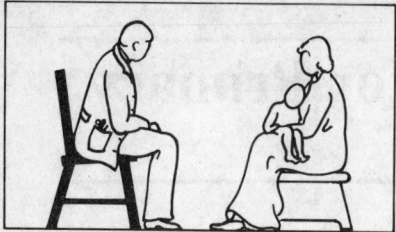

2. The 'Preventive Chair'

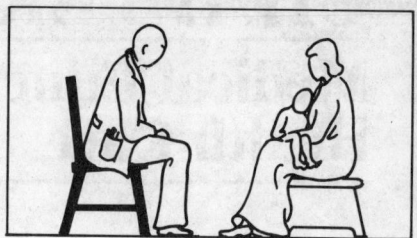

3.

COMPREHENSIVE
CHAIR

Curative and
personal
preventive
care

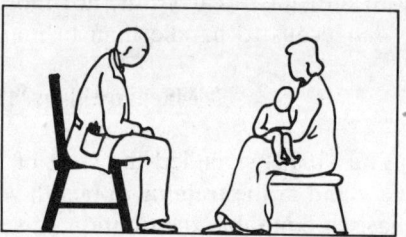

Environmental
health is the
responsibility
of the
Sanitarian

Fig. 7.1   An expanded role for the doctor within PHC

6. Working with the community in order to promote self-reliance in health.
7. Collaborating on an inter-sectoral basis with related services such as education, agriculture, public works and community development.
8. Procuring essential drugs and ensuring their availability for front line health workers.

How well is the average medical graduate prepared for fulfilling these roles? In the great majority of cases medical undergraduates in developing countries are adequately prepared for *none* of the above functions, not even that of curative care for common conditions using appropriate technology. We can characterise medical education in developing countries, with a few exceptions, as follows:

1. The training of doctors proceeds quite independently of any assessment of national manpower needs, the requirements of the health service system or the health needs of the people.
2. The curriculum has been based on that in developed industrial nations with very different traditions, health needs, material resources and socio-political and economic settings.
3. The training is hospital based rather than community oriented.
4. The training focusses on diagnosis and management of diseases, with an emphasis on rare conditions and use of high level technology for diagnosis and treatment.

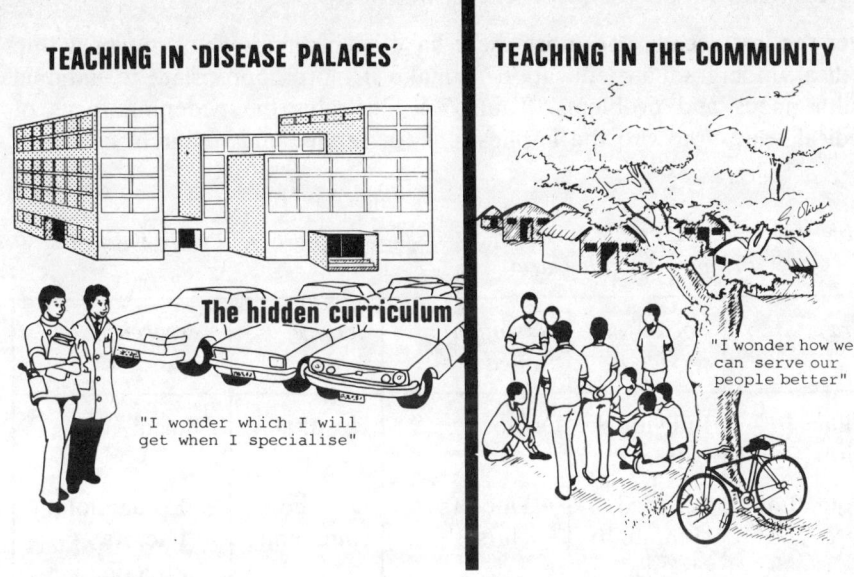

TEACHING IN 'DISEASE PALACES'

TEACHING IN THE COMMUNITY

The hidden curriculum

"I wonder which I will get when I specialise"

"I wonder how we can serve our people better"

Fig. 7.2   The 'hidden curriculum' of conventional medical schools

5.   The training gives little time to common health problems, largely ignores the promotion of health by means of preventive, promotive and rehabilitative care.
6.   The training gives virtually no time at all to planning, the management and evaluation of health services, and supervision and training of health workers.
7.   In educational approach it is discipline oriented and departmentally organised rather than competency based, problem oriented and interdisciplinary in organisation.
8.   Teaching is emphasised rather than student responsibility for learning.
9.   Very little time is devoted to working with auxiliaries and with colleagues from non-health sectors.

   The consequence of such a training is that the doctor is inappropriately prepared for dealing with the mass of the health problems in his society and unable to function effectively in situations of limited resources and with the simple technology available. The doctor is also inadequately trained for planning, managing or leading the PHC team. Frustration results. Moreover, an inappropriately trained doctor can only be harmful within the PHC system for which he is responsible. Preventive and promotive care will tend to be de-emphasised, community activity tends to be at a minimum level and other members of the team will rarely be allowed to function in the expanded PHC roles for which they have been prepared.

A widening focus for medical education

Over the last decade and more there have been a number of moves within medical undergraduate education to make it more appropriate to national health needs and problems. Table 7.1 illustrates the widening focus of medical education with the implications for service and research.

Table 7.1 The widening focus of medical education from clinical care to Primary Health Care

Era	Focus for service	Personnel trained	Service setting	Research focus
Clinical care	Individual patient	Doctors	Hospital	Clinical
Community care	Selected community groups	– Doctors – Nurses	Defined community	– Epidemiology – Factors affecting health status and service use
Primary health care	Populations	– Doctors – Nurses – Auxiliaries – Community workers	Population	– Competencies for universal coverage of population – Health services research in service delivery and management – Methods of communicating and organising communities

A number of universities and health training institutions are moving away from the emphasis on clinical care and adopting a more community care emphasis. Others are trying to use entire populations as the setting for education, service and research. In Table 7.2 some examples are given of universities and medical schools which are responding in different ways to the demands of medical education for PHC.

Table 7.2 Examples of innovative medical schools

Type of programme	Medical school
– A new medical school with a community oriented curriculum	– Aga Khan University, Karachi, Pakistan – Ben Gurion University of the Negev, Israel – Xochimilco University, Mexico City – University of Gezira, Sudan – University of Ilorin, Nigeria – Faculty of Medicine, Ramathibodi, Thailand
– A new health sciences institute as an off-shoot of an established university	– Institute of Health Sciences, Tacloban, University of the Philippines
– A new PHC curriculum in an existing medical school	– College of Medicine, University of Lagos, Nigeria
– Reorienting existing curricula towards community care and PHC	– More than 100 medical schools in India (ROME Programme) – Gadjah Mada University, Indonesia – National Autonomous University of Mexico

These schools have in common the exposing of students to health needs and problems at the community level and giving students actual responsibility for dealing with these problems. Most of the schools also have a problem based approach to learning and seek to give the students the skills and attitudes to manage with limited resources in health care delivery situations. A brief description of one programme for introducing change in medical education is provided, followed by an in-depth study of PHC training at the College of Medicine, University of Lagos. These case studies will then be utilised to illustrate some of the institutional requirements, the processes required and the problems encountered in reorienting medical education for PHC.

The UNICEF-WHO course for senior teachers of child health

In the early sixties a course for training senior academics was established at the Institute of Child Health in London with the joint sponsorship of the United Nations Children's Fund and the World Health Organisation. Every year ten paediatric academics at the middle rungs of their career were selected to attend the course of one year's duration. In the early stages the course was largely based in London with a short period of several weeks spent in developing countries, largely in tropical Africa. In 1966 the course was altered and became the London-Bombay Course with nine months in London and three months spent in Bombay. Even though field surveys were included the course remained largely academic and classroom based. In 1970 the course was restructured. The total duration was reduced to nine months, with half the time being spent in London and the other half between Sudan, East Africa and India ending with Bombay. Thus it became the UK-East Africa-India course with specific educational objectives for each centre visited. In the UK, the emphasis was largely on teaching methods, curriculum design and defining educational objectives. The participants spent four weeks at the Medical School of Newcastle upon Tyne during which period they prepared a model curriculum for their own medical school. In the Sudan, the objective was to study the training of village midwives and their work in rural areas. In East Africa, the participants studied the training of different cadres of health auxiliaries (Rural Medical Aide; MCH Aide; Medical Assistant; Assistant Medical Officer etc.) as well as their role in delivery of health care. In India, the course visited seven institutions including Jamkhed to study various aspects of training and health programmes, and carried out field surveys in a rural area and in an urban slum. By the time this course came to an end in 1978, about 140 paediatricians from the developing world had participated. Each course constituted an international forum in which common health issues were debated. Each year's group also became a travelling university from whom the host countries received as much information as was given. Currently, the participants occupy senior positions in their universities and national health services. Many have introduced innovative training and health programmes in their countries. Together they constitute a critical mass both nationally and internationally for the introduction of appropriate systems of health care and training.

Lessons learnt   The UNICEF-WHO course helped to break the mould into which medical training had been cast, and introduced new ideas of flexibility in curriculum design, as well as modern methods of teaching. Above all it helped to emphasise that medical education which does not serve the needs of the majority is of little value to the society. In its own way it helped to prepare the ground for the introduction of basic health services in the sixties and of PHC later on.

In one host country, India, the course helped to trigger a process of curriculum change which has gathered momentum and has become the national programme of Reorienting Medical Education (ROME). A travelling fellowship programme was also established along the lines of the parent course but involving largely centres in South-East Asia under the auspices of the World Health Organisation.

The experience gained from the UNICEF-WHO course has been utilised to establish a highly popular international course for training teachers of Mother and Child Health, and which leads to a Master of Science degree in the University of London.

Education for Primary Health Care in the College of Medicine, University of Lagos, Nigeria

Medical undergraduate education began in Lagos in 1962. The aim at that time was to produce doctors of international repute. The five year curriculum was modelled on those in Britain. The entire first graduating class went on to specialist studies overseas. In the mid-1970's the Nigerian government adopted the basic needs approach to health care delivery. As part of the development of the necessary teams of health workers, the medical school was directed by the government to increase its annual intake to 200 students. This extra burden stretched the human and material resources of the College to the limit. The College responded by trying to maximise the efficiency of its resources by improving teaching methods. A number of workshops on educational methods were held, supported initially by the Centre for Medical Education at the University of Dundee. Emphasis was placed on a systematic approach to medical education, seeking to develop a training programme to prepare students to meet identified needs at the level of the society. The Academic Board of the College set up a permanent curriculum review committee composed largely of senior members of faculty who had all benefitted from the medical education workshops. The committee was charged with developing a new curriculum relevant to national health needs. While this process was underway the Conference on Primary Health Care was held at Alma-Ata, in 1978, and Nigeria became a signatory to the Declaration. Thus the College was in an ideal position to incorporate the perspectives of PHC into its new curriculum which was adopted the same year. The new curriculum devotes four years to the study of basic medical and clinical sciences, and the final year to Primary Health Care. The general objectives of the revised curriculum are described in Appendix 1. The aim of the new curriculum is to increase the relevance of medical education to national health needs, in particular emphasising:
- health service coverage, especially at the level of the underserved periphery of the health system;
- preparing doctors for leadership roles within the PHC team in terms of planning, management evaluation and training functions;
- preparing doctors to function optimally in situations of scarce resources, emphasising appropriate technology.

The programme is co-ordinated by the Institute of Child Health and Primary Care, which has within it a Chair of Primary Health Care. The programme is, however, fully inter-disciplinary and eight other departments within the College of Medicine co-operate in teaching (Morbid Anatomy, Anatomy, Community Health, Preventive Dentistry, Paediatrics, Surgery,

101

Table 7.3 Primary Health Care in the Final Year programme, Lagos

Unit	Duration	Location of learning experiences	Data collection	Service	Organisation of learning (in addition to lectures)
Principles of primary care	1 week	Classroom	None	None	Group exercises
Community diagnosis	3 weeks	– Classroom – Urban community – Rural community	– Formal survey – Informal data collection from community groups and leaders	To members of community	– In pairs for field work – In groups to prepare reports
Organisation of health services	1 week	– Field visits to entire range of formal and informal health services in a community	Checklists	None	Groups
Health planning	3 weeks	Classroom	None	None	In groups preparing a health plan for the community diagnosed

Components	Duration	Setting	Evaluation	Learning methods
Components of PHC			Health status and service utilisation surveys	In each component, to appropriate target	
– Nutrition	1 week	– Classroom			– In pairs for data collection
– Immunisation	1 week	– Community			– In groups for reports
– Health education	1 week	– Local clinics			– Simulators used for FP learning experience
– Maternal	3 weeks				– Campaigns organised for immunisation
– School health	1 week				
– Child care	2 weeks				
– Primary dental care	1 week				
– Environmental sanitation	1 week				
– Treatment of common diseases	2 weeks	District hospitals General practitioners			
Management and evaluation of PHC	2 weeks	Classroom	None	None	In groups for case studies and exercises
Training of health workers	1 week	– Classroom – Community – Local clinics	None	None	Health worker training sessions conducted by group

Medicine and Obstetrics and Gynaecology). The course covers six months with a one week break at Christmas. Table 7.3 illustrates the design of the course.

The general outline of the course is to take the students through a process of community diagnosis whereby the health problems of a defined area and its level of socio-economic development are studied. Using the data generated, solutions are proposed in the health plan in such a way that the services are relevant, appropriate and can be maintained by the community in a spirit of self-reliance. These services which are largely the PHC components, are implemented by the students during the core 13 weeks of the programme. The students are also equipped with management and evaluation skills and the ability to identify needs for training in members of the health team and to organise and implement such training. The educational approach throughout is inter-disciplinary, competency and problem based and community orientated. The College of Medicine has two practice areas in use, a slum quarter of Lagos and a group of villages approximately 40 kilometres from Lagos. In both of these areas service is given at present to a defined target community, but planning and training responsibilities are being taken on for the entire Local Government Area or District. The programme places very great emphasis on fieldwork. Pairs of students are given responsibility for groups of families which they visit repeatedly over the duration of the course. The proportion of medical students from poor urban or rural backgrounds is getting less with each successive intake such that the majority now come from middle-income homes. Hence it is regarded as of central

Good health care includes home visits

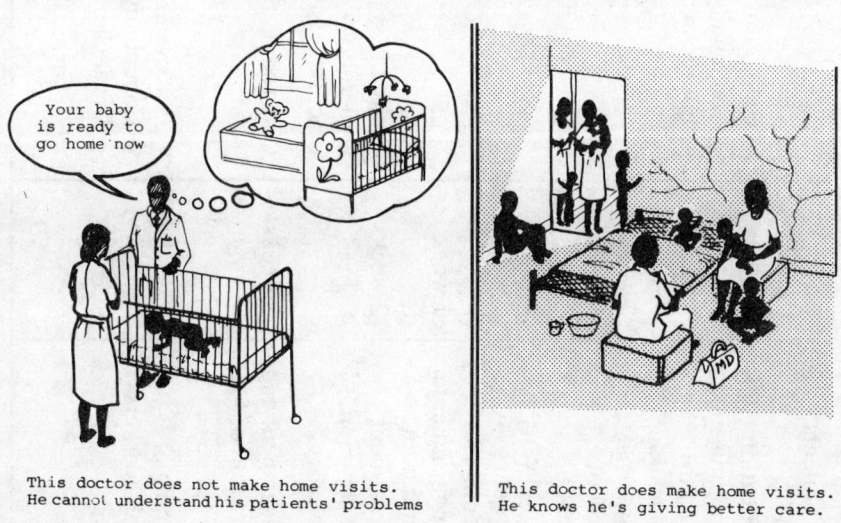

This doctor does not make home visits. He cannot understand his patients' problems

This doctor does make home visits. He knows he's giving better care.

Fig. 7.3   Working at the community level enables a comprehensive policy of health

importance to organise learning experiences at the community level such that the student builds up a comprehensive picture of the life situation as it affects the health of the majority of the population.

Medical education for PHC: the structures, processes and problems. Some lessons from Lagos and other PHC oriented medical schools

National government level

Before a substantive reorienting of medical education can take place there needs to be a statement on the part of the central government giving a clear identification of PHC as the means adopted to reach the goal of Health for All by the Year 2000. This must be backed by the allocation of necessary resources.

In Nigeria, the adoption of the basic needs approach by the government, even before Alma-Ata, began the pressure by government for medical schools to respond to the national need in the training they provided. At the same time the government began a transformation of the entire community health system through the training of new cadres of community health workers to form the nucleus of the health team. This is an extremely important step. Even the well trained PHC doctor cannot function for long without the support of an appropriately trained team. A further important government action was to allocate a capital sum to each Nigerian teaching hospital to develop a PHC centre in an underserved area. This was intended as a contribution towards more equitable distribution of services but also meant that the opportunity was created for medical schools to develop practice sites for the teaching of students. Lagos is making use of this grant to develop a PHC centre for the rural area it is currently serving by means of a variety of mobile and outreach services. In 1985 the new military government vigorously endorsed PHC as the national health strategy. By this time the College of Medicine had a well established PHC programme, having taught three successive sets of students and thus was able to take the lead as a national model for relevant and appropriate medical undergraduate education.

Institutional level

1. Existence of a permanent curriculum review mechanism The existence of a permanent curriculum review committee in Lagos greatly facilitated the revision of the curriculum and its reorientation towards PHC. It is significant also that the members of this committee, all senior members of the faculty, were already conversant with the systematic approach to education and consequently shared a common perspective on the issues involved in designing a curriculum.

105

2. Knowledge and attitude of the wider faculty about PHC   The PHC curriculum is inter-disciplinary and is the responsibility of the entire College. Considerable demands in terms of lecturing and field supervision are made on members of departments other than the co-ordinating Institute. On the whole, the wider faculty has an incomplete knowledge of PHC and of the need for a community oriented approach to teaching it. Staff members, particularly in the clinical departments, tend to resist PHC claims on their time, are somewhat resentful of the attention and resources the PHC programme attracts and fail to identify themselves with it. A weakness of the Lagos programme is that it did not educate its own faculty about PHC before attempting to educate its students. The College runs an annual medical education workshop for staff and this represents a potential opportunity to introduce PHC concepts and the community oriented approach. Even more important than communicating knowledge about PHC is the need to influence those attitudes among staff which undervalue field activities and a health care approach as distinct from disease care. There is a double need to educate the faculty about PHC because, in addition to participating in the teaching, many are also parents of medical undergraduates. Thus a distorted understanding of PHC and of the programme on their part can have damaging consequences for student morale.

A particular section of the faculty whose support is critical is the department previously called 'Public Health.' The trend in medical education is to limit the teaching of hygiene in its classical form and broaden the teaching of health at the community level, with a strong curative care content, not usually taught by Public Health Departments. A good working relationship between the teachers in the two areas (Primary Care and Public Health) is obviously essential.

3. Competency based versus subject-centred teaching   While adopting a number of innovative medical education strategies, the Lagos College of Medicine has not yet altered the traditional structure of subject based departments nor changed the system of terminal professional examinations. This has a number of adverse consequences for the PHC programme. The relative lack of understanding of the programme combined with a preference for the classical subject and examination centred approach to teaching mean that the leader of the PHC programme has to spend a considerable amount of time at the faculty committee level trying to enlist support, resist attempts to encroach on programme time and occasionally being forced to compromise with programme integrity. Concern for 'standards' means that the programme has to submit to a terminal professional examination despite a comprehensive series of in-course assessments and evaluated practical assignments.

Moreover the students find the abrupt transition from the passive learning approach of the first few years to the active responsibility for self-learning in the final year rather difficult. The students spend four years in a highly autocratic educational system and consequently take time to develop the motivation and self-discipline which the PHC learning experiences require. The implication is that the reorienting of medical education for PHC, if it is to be effective, requires a radical change in the teaching philosophy and approach of the entire medical school.

The departmental structure of the College is an obstacle in promoting an inter-disciplinary problem based approach to PHC learning. In practice, faculty members owe their primary loyalty to their department, within which basic responsibilities are assigned and promotion takes place. The demands of the PHC programme come very much in second place. An increment paid for involvement in PHC activities, as at Gadjah Mada University, might be one way of dealing with this. It has been alleged that domination of a medical school by strong subject centred departments makes innovation for PHC virtually impossible. The experience of Lagos proves it *is* possible to innovate in a traditional school but at the cost of a severe drain on the time and energy of the Primary Care Unit whose members carry an inordinately heavy load of teaching. Their research has tended to suffer in consequence, upon which career progress depends. The new Mexican University of Xochimilco also found that staff research suffered due to demands of teaching and supervising within a community oriented programme. The Aga Khan University in Karachi has adopted an innovative approach for securing teaching support. They have developed a cadre of PHC doctors called 'Preceptors' who are given a six week course to prepare them for 'precepting' groups of six to ten students in field situations. The Preceptors spend at least two days a week in the field, both in health clinics and in the community. Their training and this accumulated experience makes them effective as examples of PHC practitioners. Two innovative programmes which have developed community oriented 'tracks' are the University of New Mexico and the Autonomous National University of Mexico. Both make use of training programmes for tutors, recognising their importance as role-models for PHC students. A weakness of the Lagos programme has been its inability to develop a *group* of PHC role-models for students.

4. Role of key individuals The success of the Lagos Institute of Child Health and Primary Care in pursuing an innovative community oriented PHC programme within a traditional college owes much to the influence and personal authority of the first Director and Professor of Primary Care, a highly respected clinician of international reputation. Both Ramathibodi Faculty of Medicine and Gadjah Mada also relied heavily on charismatic leaders to launch their innovative programmes and to interpret and defend them to the wider faculty. The presence of a strong and effective leader is likely to be a crucial factor in general for the reorienting of medical education establishments.

5. Availability of a field site or practice area The skills required for PHC cannot be gained in the classroom or in the hospital. They can only be

107

acquired by means of carefully planned learning experiences in health facilities at the local level and in the community. Ben Gurion University of the Negev, in Israel, has responsibility for the health services of the Negev region. In the same way Xochimilco University in Mexico is responsible for delivery of health care to the population in the entire southern sector of Mexico City. Responsibilities at the district level are required in order to provide appropriate learning experiences and for the planning, management, evaluation and training functions of PHC. In Lagos the central government has urged the College to enlarge its responsibilities from service for a defined target community to the level of the District or Local Government Area. This is seen as constituting part of the role that the universities should play in the struggle for Health for All 2000. Actual direct responsibility for health care will continue to be exercised at the level of the smaller area. However, the College of Medicine in partnership with other departments of the University will work at the district level in strengthening the information systems for planning, managing and evaluating health services. It will also initiate reorientation and continuing education programmes for district health workers. At present administrative linkages are facilitated by personal contacts between University, State and Local Government Area personnel. For the future the organisational and managerial requirements of this kind of tripartite collaboration for PHC will need to be carefully worked out.

6. Resources to develop field sites   Many universities in the Third World already have a rural centre to which they post their students for varying periods of time. The provision of adequate learning experiences for PHC requires more than this. In particular, a community oriented approach requires a deep familiarity with the area, the people and institutions at community level. Building up this familiarity requires an active outreach activity which in turn requires appropriately trained field staff. In Lagos, a small team of field staff is largely responsible for organising the learning experiences for the students. Such a team is indispensable for realising the community oriented approach.

7. Giving curative care   Peripheral communities, denied access to health services for so long, want curative care. Curative care is also an integral part of the PHC approach. Thus the reorienting of medical education towards PHC needs to consider very carefully how the delivering of curative care can be included among the learning experiences organised at community level.

In Lagos the PHC students are in their final year and have passed the qualifying examinations at the end of the two year clinical postings. Thus they are equipped to deliver the curative care component of PHC in the community, in addition to preventive, promotive and rehabilitative care. The use of an official diagnostic and treatment manual provides legal cover for services in the community.

8. Logistic considerations for treating and service Large intakes are common in developing country medical schools. Lagos has approximately 150 in its final year class. This poses truly formidable logistic problems for organising field experiences. The greatest difficulty at present is the organisation of transport for such a large class to reach the widely dispersed sites where practical experience takes place. Vehicles and spare parts are in short supply and funds for petrol and fuel oil are limited. It is a tribute to the energy and motivation of the PHC programme leaders that despite these difficulties the programme has been able to maintain a competency based approach to learning through practical experience in the community. However, it is a continuing struggle at a time of dwindling material resources to combat the innate conservatism of the medical school that tends to favour passive learning. Active learning also consumes paper on a massive scale. The Gadjah Mada University community health programme consumed nearly 250 000 sheets of duplicating paper in a year. The total amount of paper used in Lagos each year for the PHC programme cannot be far from this. Paper is required for the course outline and statement of instructional objectives (which runs into many pages), hand-outs (in the absence of PHC textbooks), field survey materials, group exercises, case studies, continuing assessments and examinations, letters to the community preparing for field work, and so on. Active learning consumes many more resources than does 'chalk and talk' passive learning. The cost of reorienting a medical education programme towards PHC needs to be carefully estimated and appropriate provision for additional resources made when a new programme is being planned.

Service activities at community level also create a heavy demand for drugs and vaccines. In Lagos, the international agencies have supported the College with essential drugs and vaccines for PHC teaching and activities. The increase in service demand is another factor which must be considered by a medical school planning to reorient its programme.

9. Management requirements of PHC oriented medical education Community based medical education for PHC requires a supportive 'management by objectives' approach. The traditional 'administration' approach of most medical schools is not adequate to run the complex and demanding PHC programmes. It would be advisable to include administrative staff in the educational workshops on PHC so that the administrators appreciate the organisational needs for teaching. At times specially designed seminars for administrators may be needed. The potential damage that can be inflicted on a PHC educational programme by poor management or hidebound administrative regulations is so great and so frustrating that it is worthwhile investing time and effort in reorienting medical school administrators to PHC.

Contributions at the international level
A very valuable support organisation for those seeking to reorient medical

education is the Network of Community Oriented Educational Institutions for Health Sciences. This is a grouping of medical schools and health sciences institutions, half in the developed world and half in the developing world, which seeks to promote the use of a community oriented approach, problem based learning and effective teaching, learning and assessment methods. Its formation in 1979 was encouraged by the Division of Manpower Development of WHO. An interesting development is the activities of its members at the regional level. For example, Gezira University, Sudan, and Suez Canal University, Egypt, jointly run workshops for medical schools in Arab countries on educational methods, problem based learning and the community oriented approach.

Another example of bilateral co-operation to support appropriate education for PHC is that between the Autonomous University of Mexico and the University of New Mexico, USA. Both these schools are experimenting with community oriented educational 'tracks' and have exchanged students and faculty to learn from each other's experiences.

Personal contacts at the international level; faculty visits to medical schools trying innovative approaches; attendance at national and international meetings on appropriate medical education; visits by educational consultants from overseas; all these can make a decisive contribution in creating a critical proportion of the faculty prepared to try new approaches to PHC education. The sponsorship of international organisations, in particular WHO and UNICEF, has played a vital role in this regard. The donor agencies, particularly Ford and Rockefeller Foundations, have also been very supportive of universities prepared to innovate for PHC education. The Commonwealth, in its meeting of Health Ministers, has also lent its support to the need to reorient medical education. Very valuable contributions are being made by regional organisations such as the Association of Medical Schools in Africa.

Some remaining issues

1. Selection of students A few innovative schools (Tacloban, Philippines; Ben Gurion University, Israel; Ramathibodi, Thailand; the proposed school at Savar, Bangladesh) are experimenting with combining criteria such as 'rural background' and 'willingness to serve the people' with purely academic educational criteria for selection purposes. These schools also have a strong community input into the selection process. The test will be in the eventual career choices made by the graduates of these schools. However, any medical school desirous of truly reorienting its programme should consider some sort of positive discrimination in favour of underprivileged students. This is in line with the guiding principle of equity.

2. A career structure in PHC At present the graduates of the PHC programme in Lagos have no specific career structure open to them. The

110

nearest would be to take a specialist qualification in Community, or Mother and Child Health. This means that PHC is not building up a cadre of young professionals to be groomed for future PHC leadership and teaching except through a few postgraduate programmes abroad (p. 100). Thus, for the forseeable future PHC in Lagos will have to attract graduates from other professional specialities and compete with other professional loyalties.

3. Training the PHC team If we want PHC doctors to work as members of health teams they need preparation for this. The emphasis on group experience in the PHC course exposes the student to working collaboratively with other medical students. However, they are not given the experience of working with other health professionals-in-training. The training of health workers in isolation from each other has rightly been condemned as academic apartheid. The experience of schools such as Tacloban in the Philippines, which do train different levels of health worker, needs to be fully documented and shared with other PHC oriented schools, who should be urged to experiment with a team approach.

4. Continuing education for PHC Any knowledge and skill not kept up to date or shared will be lost. Continuing education is consequently a vital concern for the PHC doctor, particularly since he may well be working in a relatively isolated setting. At present the Institute of Child Health and the Postgraduate Centre in Lagos run regular one-day courses for general practitioners focussing on new advances in the management of common conditions.

THE DOCTOR WHO DOES NOT CONTINUALLY FURTHER HIS EDUCATION

Fig. 7.4   The need for life-long learning if the PHC doctor is to retain knowledge and skill

This needs to be widened to include planning, management, evaluation and training issues as well as practical 'how-to' sessions on topics such as the organisation of mass campaigns or of other community based programmes.

Conclusion

New universities and new medical schools have the great advantage of starting training for PHC because they begin with a clean slate. Existing programmes have the formidable task, which should not be underestimated, of trying to reorient an established and deeply entrenched medical education system towards PHC. Apart from anything else, the problem is on a vast scale. There are 63 medical schools in Africa, including South Africa. Only five of them (Ilorin and Lagos, Nigeria; Yaounde, Cameroun; Gezira, Sudan; and Suez Canal, Egypt) can be regarded as training appropriately for PHC. Medical teachers tend to be conservative. They also have the powerful and insidious attraction of the models and standards provided by the centres of medical excellence in the industrialised world. The call by traditional medical schools for a *maintenance of standards* amounts to an exercising of the weight of the medical establishment in the rich world to legitimise medical training and practice in the poor world. Medical education for PHC rejects this measurement of its programmes and products against the standards of the industrialised nations. Instead medical education for PHC upholds as its standard the *relevance* of the training provided for the health problems faced by the mass of the population and the efficiency of the training in producing doctors who can deal effectively with those health problems.

In Appendix I is a check-list of key questions which can serve as a guide to indicate how a given medical undergraduate training programme compares with what is required for effective PHC education. It is hoped that the experiences shared in this chapter, documented much more fully in the references overleaf, will suggest guidelines for reorientation and change. These are exciting times for the education of all types of health workers, not least the doctor.

Appendix I

Is medical education appropriate in your setting? What learning experiences do you provide to enable your graduates to think and behave in terms of:
- health rather than disease, applying techniques of prevention and health promotion as well as cure and rehabilitation
- family and community, not the sick individual alone
- membership of a health team
- making the most effective use of the financial and material resources available
- the country's pattern of health and disease and the relevant priorities

- planning, managing and evaluating the delivery of health services
- identifying training needs among members of the health team and implementing such training
- working in partnership with local communities to improve health

If NOT, what is required to improve the situation?

- actions on part of Ministry of Health and/or Ministry of Education?
- organising workshops in medical education and PHC to bring about a change in knowledge and attitudes on the part of faculty members and the medical school administration?
- a change in student attitudes?
- providing a field practice site at the level of an entire peri-urban or rural community?
- setting up necessary administrative arrangements?
- other changes peculiar to your setting?

Source: adapted from WHO Forum (1985).

Appendix II

The general objectives of the new curriculum, College of Medicine, University of Lagos, Nigeria
At the end of the medical undergraduate programme the student should possess:

A Knowledge of
1. the normal structure, function, development and growth of the human body, mind and society;
2. the disorders of structure, functions, development and growth of the human body, mind and society that occur as a result of ill-health;
3. appropriate measures (promotive, preventive and curative) that can be used to identify and solve the health problems of individuals, families and communities.

B Ability (skills) to
1. collect, record and evaluate data about the health needs of individuals, families and communities;
2. recognise (diagnose) the health problems of individuals, families and communities;
3. utilise appropriate measures (promotive, preventive and curative) in the solution of health problems of individuals, families and communities;
4. express himself (in the appropriate language) fluently and unambiguously about the health needs of individuals, families and communities;
5. find and critically evaluate literature about health matters.

C The following attitudes:
1. appreciation that medical education does not end with completion of the

undergraduate course, and acceptance of full responsibility for continuing his own education;

2. the habit to look at any health problem, whether of an individual, a family or a community, comprehensively and in its total environment;
3. determination to observe at all times high ethical standards in the practice of his profession;
4. awareness of the scope and limits of his role and of the necessity to seek and use regularly the collaboration of other health workers;
5. a high sense of responsibility towards work and calmness in emergency situations;
6. readiness to evaluate critically the results of utilising measures as required in 1–5 above, and carry out simple, problem orientated research according to scientific principles;
7. readiness to plan, manage and evaluate health services for individuals, families and communities;
8. readiness to educate, motivate, supervise and lead other health workers in health promotion and the prevention and treatment of disease;
9. in respect of all the skills stated above, willingness to function optimally, critically and innovatively even when manpower and other resources are limited.

Further reading

1 Training of health personnel for PHC in general

Fülöp, T., 'Trends in the education of health personnel worldwide', (1978) in McNeur, R.W. (Ed), *The changing roles and education of health personnel in view of the increase of basic health services*, Philadelphia: Society for Health & Human Values, 1978.

Katz, F.M. and Fülöp, T., *Personnel for Health Care: Case studies of educational programmes*, Public Health Papers Nos. 70–71, Geneva: World Health Organisation (including Tacloban, Xochimilco and Ben Gurion Universities), 1978.

Sebai, Z.A., *Role of hospitals in training and orienting physicians and other health professionals towards PHC*, Conference on Role of Hospitals in PHC, sponsored by Aga Khan Foundation and WHO, Pakistan, 1981.

2 Specific medical school programmes

Buri, P. et al, 'The Ramathibodi community health programme', *J. Med. Educ.*, 49, 264–277, 1974.

Northrup, R.S. and Rohde, J.E., *Teaching community medicine to doctors: Observations on the Gadjah Mada experience*, Mimeo, 1977.

Smilkstein, G., 'Medical education in Indonesia: Primary Care and Community Health', (Udayana University, Bali), *J. Med. Educ.* 57, 5, 386–392, 1982.

Cortes, M.T. et al, 'Community-oriented medical education: comparison of tracks in Mexico and New Mexico', *Med. Educ.* 19, 199–207, 1985.

Ekunwe, E.O. and Johnson, T.O., *The Lagos experience of Primary Health Care in the curriculum for medical students*, WHO/CAMAS Workshop on the Orientation of Medical Training and Medical Teachers towards Primary Health Care, Cotonou, Benin Republic, 1985.

3 Medical schools and PHC

Round Table: 'Wanted a new breed of doctors', *WHO Forum*, 6, 4, 291–309, 1985.

Greep, J.M. and Schmidt, H.G., 'The Network (of community-oriented health training institutions)', *World Health*, April, 18–21, 1984.

Solanke, T.F., *Orientation of medical training and medical teachers towards Primary Health Care*, WHO/CAMAS Workshop, Cotonou, Benin Republic, 1985.

Commonwealth Secretariat, *The contribution of medical schools to national health development*, Report of a workshop prepared for the 7th Commonwealth Health Ministers Meeting, Ottawa, Canada, (HMM 83/WS/2), 1983.

Primary Health Care in undergraduate medical education, Report of a WHO meeting, Exeter 18th–22nd July, Copenhagen: WHO Regional Office for Europe, 1983.

Stuart, K., 'Health for All: Its challenge for medical schools', *The Lancet*, Feb 25, 441–442, 1984.

4 Universities and PHC

Akinkugbe, O.O., 'Ivory tower or social commitment', *World Health*, April, 2–3, 1984.

Akinkugbe, O.O., 'Universities and Health for All, *World Health Forum* 5, 1, 3–4, 1984.

Akinkugbe, O.O., Forum Interview: *Universities in developing countries*, WHO Forum 5, 4, 348–353, 1984.

Wray, J.D., 'Undergraduate and graduate education in community medicine', in Lathem, W. and Newberry, A., *Community Medicine: Teaching, Research and Health Care*, New York, Appleton-Century Crofts, 1970.

115

CHAPTER 8
Nursing Models for Primary Health Care

The orientation of nursing towards PHC can only be carried out within existing local political and economic systems. Hitherto a sense of paternalism has been conveyed by terms like the 'Third World Nurse'. Such a notion has so far served to provide a convenient peg on which more developed countries have hung a restatement of established practices in the planning of nursing services. It has also acted as an inhibiting factor in introducing change towards PHC. Many would say that it has helped more developed countries to maintain the status quo within political systems which identify health care needs on the basis of a developed economy. The need for nursing to reorientate towards PHC is therefore as urgent as in physician education in order to match the challenge of the local health needs. It is the purpose of this chapter to describe some current models which determine the practice of nursing across cultures and in varied settings. In particular the close relationship between the elements of PHC and the core components of nursing are examined to offer a redefinition of nursing within which strategies for reorientation towards PHC can be found.

Issues in professional orientation of nurses

Few nursing education programmes prepare nurses for the realities which will confront them at work. Firstly, the resources get severely limited, the more they move to the front line. Secondly, what strikes many nurses when they start work in a clinic or hospital is how busy it is. In an overcrowded hospital ward with many acutely ill patients or in a busy clinic there is hardly any scope for putting into practice what they learnt about communication, management, family counselling, and so on. If they do any home visiting they quickly despair of any potential for change when they see the grim truth of poverty which afflicts a majority of the population. Thirdly, most of the patients they see in a clinic are suffering from preventable illnesses. Worst of all they see the same people with recurrent illness so aptly described as the 'revolving-door' situation, i.e. the same patient attending periodically with an infective illness and going away with possibly the same medicine.

They often find that few people are able to follow the teaching they have spent so much time communicating. It is one thing to talk about feeding triple-mixes or raising the energy density of weaning foods by the addition of oil, and another whether people actually have those substances at home.

The requirements for professional practices in such a situation demand that nurses and other health workers should be trained to work in the ecological setting of the country. Reorientation towards PHC is possible once appropriate training strategies are adopted. The starting point for developing such an approach is the redefinition of nursing in relation to existing needs and resources and a re-examination of the potential of the nurses as health workers in the context of the environment. Let us take one example.

Evidence from a number of countries suggests that the distribution of deaths in young children over a given period are concentrated in a relatively small number of households. Among these will be a hard core of families who currently receive little or no health care at all. These isolated, vulnerable, poor and ill-supported families suffer the most deaths of children.

Service based approaches to primary health care benefit the majority of families in which child death is an isolated or rare occurrence because these families have the resources and support to follow the advice given. However, such approaches have little effect on those with high mortality. Health 'messages' which encourage the use of salt and sugar in water for treating diarrhoea simply have no meaning in poverty-stricken families. Nurses must be trained to play a much more problem oriented, flexible and learning role to overcome such problems.

This, in turn, will require a more responsive and supportive system. This is crucial. A nurse can work only in an environment that supports fully what he or she has been trained to do. If nursing education merely 'adds' a couple of sessions on primary health care to a syllabus that is already overcrowded with facts vital to pass examinations based on a Western syllabus, then the concept of primary health care does not stand a chance. If a nurse is to support the smooth running of primary health care in a nearby community but is meanwhile running a desperately busy clinic, it is likely that the latter will take priority. If nursing education merely equips nurses to deliver 'appropriate messages' to a community which is seen as a homogenous mass of people with equal resources and support, then only those in possession of the resources and support will benefit.

Realising these difficulties countries have evolved a variety of strategies for the orientation of nurse training towards PHC. A case study from the **Caribbean** illustrates one of these.

The Schools of Nursing in the Caribbean have been seeking to move nursing education into health science centres or colleges of education. This was one way of breaking the mould and getting nurse training out of the rut. There followed a process of curriculum development through the following steps:

1. A policy statement, most often in the form of a request from the Ministry of Health asking for a review and readjustment of the curriculum of the school of nursing so as to be relevant to PHC.
2. Establishment of a curriculum committee with defined terms of reference. The membership of the committee was made deliberately wide to include members of the Nursing Council, representatives of the community, of the education department, of different aspects of the nursing service as well as the teaching staff of the nursing school. A core committee then took on the specific responsibilities of curriculum development and reported back to the general committee.
3. Development of a plan of work with defined targets for completion of work and data gathering.
4. The relevant data gathered were utilised for developing teaching strategies, students' learning experiences and for developing course content.

As a result of the above exercise the content of nursing education in the Caribbean is becoming organised around the basic needs at different stages of the life-cycle, and focusses on the factors in the physical, biological, psycho-social and the cultural-political environment which affect each stage. The major health problems of the individual country form the models for the content of the nursing studies, as well as the bases for students' projects. Some of the important concepts of PHC like maternal and child health; nutrition, programmes of immunisation and oral rehydration; health education; community participation; inter-sectoral collaboration and so on are woven into this approach to learning. Such an educational strategy fosters problem oriented learning whilst being more relevant to the health needs of the country. The types of courses offered in this new curriculum are shown in Table 8.1.

Table 8.1 The Caribbean project for the development of the nursing curriculum

I Nursing courses
1. Evolution of nursing.
2. The well individual and his family.
3. Concepts related to nursing.
4. Basic needs of the pre-school child. Factors affecting these needs.
5. Basic needs of the school child and his family. Factors affecting these needs.
6. Basic needs of the adolescent, the young adult and the family.

Factors affecting these needs (to include MCH).

7. Basic needs of the middle aged and older adult and family. Factors affecting these needs.
8. Basic needs of the elderly and the family. Factors affecting these needs.
9. Professional development:
   - management/administration
   - career development
   - research
   - principles of teaching.
10. Special nursing: operating room, intensive care unit, emergency nursing and disaster preparedness and management.

II Support courses

1. First aid.
2. Integrated sciences (human biology, biochemistry and biophysics).
3. Basic psychology ⎰ including community development. ⎱
4. Basic sociology
5. Microbiology.
6. Nutrition.
7. Pharmacology (including traditional medicines).
8. Pathophysiology.
9. Agricultural science.

A definition of nursing

The change in nursing education in the Caribbean is a good example of what can be achieved through regional co-operation. Such a new ferment is necessary because existing definitions of nursing are related to the needs of developed societies whence the nursing profession evolved. However, the definition of the role of nurses offered by Henderson (1966) has a universal appeal. According to her the unique function of the nurse is to assist the individual (sick or well) in the performance of those activities which he or she would perform unaided if capable of doing so. Accordingly fourteen basic principles which are related to the activities of living are described; for example the ability to eat, breathe, wash, and generally to live normally. Where the performance of such natural activities is impaired due to physical, psychological or environmental factors, the nurse assists the individual to carry them out. This definition would normally apply to all settings where nursing takes place. This definition can be expanded in terms of PHC as follows:

'Nursing is a caring approach to the needs of individuals, families and groups comprising all elements which enable individuals and groups to adapt to health care needs within their environment.'

Health needs of individuals and communities change over time, and so do the perceptions of such needs as well as strategies for fulfilling them. Hence change is the key word in planning nursing strategies. This applies also to the new perceptions which have grown out of the drive for PHC. Fig. 8.1 is a planning model for developing nursing strategies responsive to PHC.

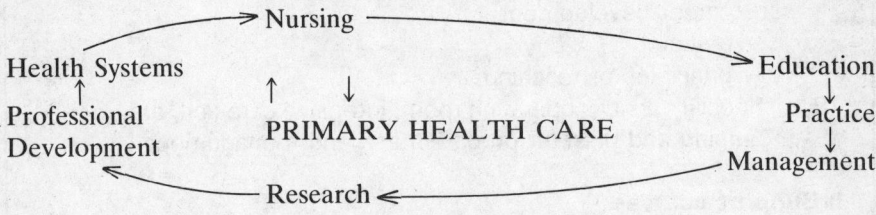

Fig. 8.1   Planning model for developing nursing strategies

Two models of nursing practice

Although nursing has a universal base as defined by Henderson (1966) its practice is locally identified. In most countries nursing has developed within inappropriate health systems resulting in a service which is curative and subservient to the medical profession. In order to develop an alternative understanding of nursing strategies for PHC it may be useful to consider two more recent and widely accepted models of nursing. These models help to underpin the theoretical justification of nursing as a professional practice. The importance of these models lies in the fact that:
1. They have approached a universal application since they are based on knowledge derived from the biological and behavioural sciences.
2. The use of models in any case enables the nurse to plan care based on appropriate rationale for individual needs of clients.
3. They are an advance on previous models, and pave the way for nursing models which are more appropriate for PHC.

Orem's self-care model

Orem's Model was introduced in 1971. It formed one of several basic theoretical foundations for professional nursing practice.

Eight elements are defined by Orem in relation to normal human experience and the need for care. These are summarised as follows:
1. Maintenance of a sufficient intake of air (Respiration)
2. Maintenance of sufficient intake of water (Osmo-regulation)
3. Maintenance of sufficient intake of food (Nutrition)

4. The provision of care associated with elimination processes (Excretory)
5. Maintenance of a balance between activity and rest (Rehabilitatory)
6. Maintenance of a balance between solitude and social interaction (Psycho-social)
7. The prevention of hazards to human life, functioning and well-being
8. The promotion of human functioning and development within social groups in accordance with individual potential, known limitations and desire to be 'normal'.

Elements 1, 2, 3, and 4 correspond to important aspects of biological homeostasis. On the other hand, 5, 6, 7 and 8 have within them components relevant to all aspects of activities of living. But the model needs to be developed further for it to apply to communities in the developing world. It would need to take account of ecology and epidemiology and belief systems in the interest of PHC. It needs the following additions:

9. Basic systems of care for individuals

Orem is concerned fundamentally with the notion of care. She suggested that it is a universal truth that individuals care for themselves and, when unable to do so, nurses and other workers substitute for this deficit viz. the inability to perform self-care. According to the principles of PHC nurses and other health workers act as 'enablers' i.e. enabling communities to care for themselves.

Orem identifies three basic care systems as follows:
a) A wholly compensatory system of care.
b) A partly compensatory system of care.
c) A supportive-educative system of care.

Categorising care needs of individuals
In the context of practical nursing these systems may be further considered as follows:
(a) A wholly compensatory care is one that is required by an individual who is unable to manage life activities without assistance.
    Examples of such a situation are:
    − Acute physically or emotionally ill person.
    − The critically injured and unconscious individual.
    − Severely disturbed individual with emotional problems.
    − Post-operative unconscious patients in intensive care units.
b) Partly compensatory care is that which is required by an individual in order to cope with restorative or therapeutic aspects of life activities. This suggests that some degree of self-care is generally present but an optimum level for the maintenance of homeostasis may not be attained unless assistance is given. The nurse is professionally prepared to give such assistance. Examples of this type of care are readily observed in hospital and community care.
c) The supportive-educative care system is designed to assist the individual in efforts to achieve a certain level of self-care commensurate with the

121

optimum level for homeostasis. However, because of some limitations to achieving a total self-care independently, nurses or other health workers provide supportive and educative assistance.

Thus, it can be seen that by using this model, it is possible to organise nursing support based on a conceptual framework of self-care. Thus care plans may be considered from the point of view of Orem's eight universal requisites and a decision made as to which of the three identified systems of care is appropriate to individual need. The application of this model has some value in planning nursing strategies for PHC in the developing world. This is because the concept of self-care involves self-education, and professional skills are needed to assist individuals and communities in rural and urban areas to maintain self-care. In order to meet the needs of people in sickness and in health within the primary health care context, the nurse must have an adequate knowledge base for practice.

The use of Orem's model is one approach; the second approach to be considered is Roy's Adaptation Model.

Roy's Adaptation Model

The Roy Adaptation Model is one of a series of theories developed in the United States in the 1970s. The link between theory and practice is an important consideration in nursing and this model makes a fundamental contribution to the development of an appropriate theoretical framework for nursing practice.

Roy's model is concerned with the problem of *human adaptation*. It is based on a biological system model. According to this model the human organism consists of parts which depend for their existence on an integrated functioning of the whole body. The parts which make up the whole, it is argued, are linked together in a dynamic equilibrium such that changes in one part may lead to a reaction which ultimately affects the whole organism. The forces of disequilibrium may be biological, psychological or sociological. Hence the view that man is a bio-psycho-social being who is in continuing interaction with his environment and adapting to it as appropriate. This concept, viz. that of homeostasis, is fundamental to this theory of nursing.

Summary of the model's underlying principles
1. Man is viewed as a 'bio-psycho-social' being. It is from this premise that the idea of holistic care i.e. individualised, personalised care developed.
2. Man is fundamentally an interactionist. It is suggested that man needs and indeed seeks intellectual, physical and social stimulations. The maintenance of man's psychological and social well-being depends on how successful he is in this process of interaction with his environment and his fellow beings.
3. Physiological and ecological changes occur within and outside the human organism and, in order to cope with these, homeostatic mechanisms

exist which maintain and sustain the processes that ensure survival through adaptation.

4. Health and illness are important concepts in the study of man. They are part of the continuum of human existence and experience as a living being.
5. Biologically, the body's genetic constitution determines its ability to adapt to changes within and outside the body. This innate capability is, however, affected by an individual's psychological and social situation. Hence, it is reasonable to suggest that individual responses to these changes differ and reflect general and environmental factors.
6. Adaptation − this is the key concept in Roy's model. It is argued that human adaptive response is zonal. This means that the body is regarded as consisting of various zones for the reception of stimuli. Thus when a stimulus falls within a particular zone in the body, it excites a response whereas if the same stimulus falls outside the particular zone, no response would be excited. This would seem important for survival. It is supported by the physiological notion of specialised sensory arrangement whereby visual stimulation is responded to by the eyes while sound stimulus is responded to by the auditory apparatus.

Application of Roy's Adaptation Model

A theory or a model is a means to an end. It provides a theoretical framework for the planning of nursing care. Roy's model has been widely used in curriculum development in the United States and also clinically, for example in the care of the elderly. For developing countries Roy's model provides a basis for professional interventions. Because PHC depends both on individuals and team work amongst those providing care the use of a model helps to identify areas of important needs for the maintenance of health.

Roy's Adaptation Model is a practical framework for assessment, planning, implementation and evaluation of nursing care. In the orientation of nursing strategies towards PHC it has some value, provided the cultural, religious and belief systems are also taken into account for planning.

The two models described above provide different ways of looking at the role of the nurse. Whilst 'self-care' and 'adaptation' are universal concepts and provide useful theoretical frameworks, the two models were essentially designed with the more developed world in mind. They fall short of the reality of the developing world where the main challenge is survival. Modern nursing texts based on these models are also inappropriate for the education of nurses in the developing world. Hence a new approach which addresses the notion of survival as the central theme needs to be evolved.

A 'survival' model for planning nursing care

In the developing world the major challenge for the nurse or PHC worker is to assist the individuals and communities in the struggle for survival. In this struggle individuals need to be helped to identify those elements which enable them to interact with their environment in a positive manner. Interventions must be directed towards fulfilling the survival needs of individuals, families and communities.

Factors inhibiting change in nursing

Change means a reorientation towards a health system which relocates resources to help meet the needs of a local community irrespective of its environmental setting. The key elements in this consideration are the ability to adapt, as well as the resources available for such adaptation. Another essential element to consider is the need to abandon what might be termed the 'missionary' approach to the delivery of health care in developing countries. By this we mean the way in which local responses to needs are conditioned by external factors. This is not to say that the missionary approach is entirely worthless, but what seems to be inappropriate is the way in which what we call the 'dependency factor' dominates the relationship between the local communities and the so-called care givers. Very often the care giver is part of the aid structure of a developed country and may therefore bring a further inhibiting factor to change, that is a personal feeling of power so that the care giving system comes to dominate over local initiatives which may be more appropriate.

Because of its covert dominance over local initiatives this approach may serve to inhibit real progress in terms of reorientation towards PHC.

Amongst the factors which inhibit change, the following examples illustrate some of the important ones.

1. The system as an inhibiting factor

The socio-political and economic infrastructures of a society determine the various outcomes of change. This makes the individual less able to facilitate change because the motivation required to effect change must operate against certain vested interests. These are usually exceedingly powerful within society and, in the case of developing countries, are linked to external systems. Inevitably therefore, politico-economic factors are at the heart of the inability of the individual to effect change. Any attempt to change the educational provision for nurses must be supported by the political system. Project 2000 in Britain was an attempt to redefine the educational needs of British nurses so that community care becomes an integral part of the preparation for professional practice. However, the health system which is determined by the political vision of the party in power must support change in nursing education if it is to be effected. In practice, there are a number of factors which prevent such support being given. If the government is not supportive of change, neither the individual nor the profession can move forward. Historically, the power of the State to resist change is demonstrated by the myriads of reports the recommendations of which have neither seen the light of day nor led to any changes in nursing education in Britain.

If the nursing profession in Britain has experienced difficulties reorienting its own educational system, it seems reasonable to argue that developing countries ought not to depend on it to provide a lead.

In developing countries strong governmental control can inhibit change within nursing systems. Allied to this is the influence of groups within the health care system often the most powerful being the medical profession.

2. The individual as an inhibiting factor

We cannot consider individuals in isolation since their ideas on health are influenced by their beliefs, personal philosophy and perceptions of the world. These may either enhance or inhibit the way health is perceived. Individuals also operate within established health systems.

Focus on nursing strategies for PHC

The role of nurses in the implementation of PHC is now widely recognised as crucial. It is also important to think beyond the year 2000 and evolve plans to focus on long-term provision of nursing care. Such plans should develop along a national and international framework (Table 8.2).

Table 8.2 Framework for managing health – focus on PHC nursing strategies

Identified strategy	Focus for implementation	Comments
International	WHO policies; UN agencies; European Economic Community; The Commonwealth and aid agencies; Non-aligned countries; USSR and satellite countries.	Impact of the philosophies of pressure groups and change agents.
National	Elite/Disadvantaged; Developed/Underdeveloped; The so-called 'Third World'.	National Aid Programme; Technical Exchange; Dynamics of Trade.
Health Systems	Political orientation of the nurse as health worker; Infrastructure for the provision of health care.	Education of the nurse. Social policy implications.

Within such a large framework attention needs to be focussed on the individual, the family group, and the community. It is at this micro level that the nurse is being recognised as a key health worker.

Elements within PHC relevant to nursing strategies

Two key elements may be identified as relating to the contribution of nurses to PHC. These are health promotion and health maintenance, in both of which nurses play the role of enablers. In no other service is this better seen than in the case of maternal and child health (MCH). In countries where people under the age of 15 and women in the reproductive period of life together make up two-thirds of the population, such services are extremely important. Health promotion, surveillance and counselling form the key elements of the MCH services, the objective of which is to maintain the individual in good health from conception to maturity. Moreover, the MCH services are largely concerned with family formation, and so those who work in MCH are closely involved with families and the maintenance of their health. Thus the nurse is the grass roots worker putting the elements of UNICEF's GOBI programme into action. Similarly most of the elements of PHC besides MCH fall in the domain of nursing. Hence national strategies for both PHC and GOBI cannot succeed without the support of the nursing services. In fact the nursing profession is well placed in most countries to lead the way to reorientation of the health services towards PHC.

Challenges for the future

A number of demographic, social and political processes together with professional insight create special challenges for nursing. Most important is the demographic change creating special needs for health coverage in the developing world. The demographic change is of two kinds viz. population growth and population movement.

1. *Population growth*   In countries where up to 80 per cent of the people live in rural areas most population growth is in the countryside. Hence the need for expanding rural health services.
   Countries are responding to the health demands in a number of ways as illustrated by the following examples:
   – Reorientation and expansion of nursing training and the training of a new cadre of community health nurse, for example **Kenya**.

Kenya has introduced a new syllabus lasting four years for training the Kenyan Registered Community Nurse. On completion of the course the graduate is intended to function as a general nurse, a midwife and a community health nurse besides being able to deal with common psychiatric problems.

The Kenya Enrolled Nursing Course, which was started in 1959, used to train nurses mainly for curative type of work. In order to satisfy the growing demand of community nursing like MCH, Family Planning and front line health care the Enrolled Community Nursing

Programme was started in 1966. The graduates are able to function as community midwives, ward nurses or public health nurses as the need may be, in accordance with the integrated rural health services in Kenya.

The Kenya Registered Public Health Nursing Course started in 1972 to provide postgraduate training to those nurses who have had at least five years' work experience. On qualification the participants work in a supervisory capacity putting their skills in community diagnosis, health education and preventive medicine to work.

— Creating new cadres of front line workers for example **Tanzania**.

Tanzania commenced a new programme of training MCH aides in the seventies channelling national resources into building 19 training schools for MCH aides in preference to the proposed expansion of the medical school. The graduates, who are primary school leavers and go through a training programme of 18 months, work in rural clinics providing MCH care. Tanzania could not possibly have achieved the coverage with antenatal and maternity services as well as for immunisation as she does today without expanding the cadre of such front line workers.

2. *Population movements*   Urbanisation is a major challenge in the developing world, with some cities experiencing unprecedented growth of their population. New approaches and concepts will need to be evolved to provide health care to squatter populations living in the septic fringes of the cities. Concepts like the village health worker, community health volunteer and traditional birth attendant are being adapted to fit the needs of the urban populations. The existence of established front line cadres like Enrolled Community Nurse (Kenya), MCH Aides (Tanzania), Auxiliary Nurse Midwives (India) and so on will provide the nucleus for Community Health Nursing combining the skills of nursing, public health and social assistance. Such a nucleus of community health nursing in each neighbourhood will create the resources needed for the care of well families, combining it with ambulatory care and care of groups like the elderly, the disabled and the emotionally disturbed. In addition support will be given to public health programmes that affect the whole community.

Resource constraint is another factor affecting the strategies of health services development in all countries. This is especially so in relatively small countries like Nepal, Bhutan, Botswana, the Gambia and so on. The national economies as well as the relatively small size of their population makes the building of medical schools uneconomical. Traditionally these countries have depended on their larger neighbours for the training of physicians and specialists, which understandably has not been satisfactory. Several countries are responding to the growing demand for physicians by training nurse practitioners. Kenya has had a longstanding programme of training nurses with several years' experience as clinical officers. Health centres and dispensaries are run largely by such clinical officers who are the counterparts of Tanzania's medical assistants and rural medical aides.

In the seventies, **Botswana** began the planning of a one-year post-basic programme of training Family Nurse Practitioners (FNP). At independence in 1965 there were no indigenous physicians in the country, most medical care being provided by expatriate missionaries. The FNP programme may be looked upon as continuing education for nurses dealing with ambulatory care. On the other hand it may be viewed as a response to the need for health personnel in the country's strategy for expanding health services.

In summary, this chapter has looked at some conceptual models and frameworks within which the nursing profession can be oriented towards PHC. The 'enabler' function on which professional nursing practice is based makes the nurse a key health worker in the global strategy of achieving Health for All by the Year 2000. A number of elements within PHC are closely associated with the task of enabling individuals, families and communities to care for themselves. Reorientation of nursing strategies towards PHC is already on its way in many countries.

Further reading

Aggleton, P. and Chalmers, H., *Nursing Models and the Nursing Process*, London, Macmillan, 1986.

Akinsanya, J.A., 'The uses of theories of nursing', Occasional Papers, *Nursing Times*, 80: 59–60, 1984.

Chinn, P.L., *Advances in Nursing Theory and Development*, Rockville, Maryland, Aspen Publication, 1983.

Henderson, V., *The Nature of Nursing*, London, Collier Macmillan, 1966.

Orem, D.E., *Nursing: Concepts of Practice*, Second Edition, New York, McGraw-Hill, 1980.

Pearson, A. and Vaughan, B., *Nursing Models for Practice*, London, Heinemann, 1986.

Riehl, J.P. and Roy, C., *Conceptual Models for Nursing Practice*, (2nd Edition) Norwalk, Appleton-Century Croft, 1980.

The Nursing Theories Conference Group, *Nursing Theories: the base for processional nursing practice*, Englewood Cliff, New Jersey, Prentice-Hall Inc., 1980.

United Kingdom Central Council for Nursing, *Midwifery and Health Visiting*, Project 2000, London UKCC, 1986.

World Health Organisation, *Global Strategy for Health for All by the Year 2000*, Geneva WHO, 1981.

CHAPTER 9
Intersectoral Collaboration

'Local (district) health personnel interacting with officials from other agencies (agriculture, public works, community development and education, for example), and with representatives of political structures and the general population, are often better placed to find workable responses to local problems than higher-placed officials in the national capital.'

UNICEF/WHO Joint Committee on Health Policy, 1981

A great number of illnesses can be avoided by measures other than curative health care. Such measures may be in the general developmental sector like improved supplies of food and water, environmental sanitation and vector control. In the educational sector such measures include raising the awareness of parents regarding health, nutrition and agriculture. Measures in the sector of community development include increasing employment opportunity, income generation, raising the general standard of living and alleviation of women's work load through appropriate technology. Sadly, the old pattern of planning still continues in many countries so that the massive burden of preventable diseases continues to be tackled through classical disease-centred health services. The result is that enormous demands are being made on the scarce financial and skilled resources without breaking the vicious circle of disease → treatment → recurrence.

The effectiveness of PHC is greatly reduced if the general living conditions of the community are not improved in an equitable manner. For example, nutrition education by itself is meaningless if the conditions of daily life and the socio-political structures allow only those better off to implement the knowledge. On the other hand, increased income may not necessarily result in nutrition and health improvement. Prestigious consumer goods may be preferred to basic necessities; cash received from home grown vegetables and milk from the family cow may be spent on aerated drinks and junk foods; dietary intake may change from the local staple to imported cereals like wheat flour or polished rice. There are instances where health status has actually declined in the wake of relatively rapid economic growth particularly among the poor. This is because of the failure to counteract negative effects of economic growth as in the case of the Green Revolution, for example.

Tracing the links between development and health

The links between development and health are complex but fairly well known. In developed countries the communicable diseases which were the main causes of mortality were controlled more by improvements in general living conditions, improved nutritional status, sanitation and health behaviour than by major discoveries for their cure and treatment. In developing countries, however, improvement in health is closely linked with strategies for meeting the basic needs of the population. This entails giving the poor access to resources and economic opportunities, raising educational levels, ensuring availability of food, improving the status of women, and providing the basic infrastructure of services.

Within the various development sectors are found complex factors which influence health and ill-health. Economic development by itself may even be counter-productive for health unless carefully planned, for example, agricultural policies which favour cash crops but may affect food availability; large irrigation projects which increase agricultural output but which can also become major transmitters of disease; and industrial projects which increase environmental pollution.

Within recent years there has been growing recognition that improved health should be a major goal of the development process. The changing health situation of a country provides one of the most revealing indicators of the quality of its development. Strategies for national development can influence a country's health situation through their impact on income distribution. They can correct the bias between urban and rural areas. National health statistics do not always reveal the disparities between urban and rural areas. In Peru, for example, in rural highland areas infant mortality has averaged 127/1000 live births, but in isolated rural communities the rate reaches 500/1000 − or one death in every two live births. Development strategies are needed which give priorities to vulnerable groups (for example Costa Rica page 12 and India page 10).

Current trends in policy-making and planning

Although much 'lip service' is paid to the benefits of integrated social, cultural and economic development, many developing countries continue to pursue single-track policies for economic growth. As a result, resources are heavily concentrated on investment in the modernisation and expansion of production. Social objectives are given a low priority as their positive impact on production cannot be readily proved. Poverty, crowding, endemic and epidemic diseases are treated as the unavoidable price of economic progress. So far the health sector has only played a remedial role to counteract the adverse effects of such development policies. This is partly due to lack of collaboration between industrial and health planning.

Despite endorsement by many countries of the PHC policies, health planning has generally remained the responsibility of the health sector alone. This isolation is reinforced by the continued perception of health as mainly medical services and their output. This pushes the health strategy back to a curative approach. In this context other sectors regard health as the business of the health sector alone and intersectoral co-operation as a diversion of time and resources from their own sectoral priorities and goals. This is largely so because the system for development planning normally organises activities vertically, neglecting horizontal links which can have synergistic impact on development. Also, mechanisms for intersectoral action and co-ordination may not exist.

Effective health policies need to identify early the possible health risks within the policies of other sectors. The latter need to incorporate goals of health improvement into their own sectoral goals and to be clear about the health implications of their own policies.

Mechanisms for intersectoral collaboration

Various institutional mechanisms have been introduced by countries for intersectoral co-operation and co-ordination. For example, National Health Councils which bring together representatives of many agencies and groups may be convened by the highest levels of government and include Ministers, as for example in Sri Lanka. These may be sub-committees of a national intersectoral agency like a planning commission or a developmental council, such as in the Republic of Korea; or they may be initiated by the Ministry of Health itself. Such councils provide political support for intersectoral co-ordination. They have the information and national perspective needed for general policy co-ordination. Technical resources for top-level intersectoral co-ordination may also be provided by a national health development net-work. Such a network links existing institutions relevant to health: such as ministries, universities, research institutes, labour organisations, development agencies and non-governmental agencies. This network can formulate policy options, or propose intersectoral strategies.

Network participation of health training institutions is particularly important since their staff can encourage intersectoral thinking in training the next generation of health workers.

Regional, district and village level councils link state and local government officials to representatives of Ministries of Health and other ministries. Networks formed at these levels have been used to plan, implement and monitor intersectoral projects. The composition and management of such a network calls for considerable interpersonal and political skill. Decentralisation of the Ministry of Health and other sectors can enable local government officials to play a larger role in co-ordinating different agencies.

In some countries political party organisations are important supports to intersectoral co-ordination. Parties with well developed 'grass-roots' organisations can put pressure on bureaucracies for better co-ordinated services, as has occurred in Mozambique, or in Ghana through people's defence committees exerting pressure at village level.

Structures of participation forged during the independence struggle may continue to provide channels for popular involvement after independence as in the case of FRELIMO (Mozambique) and TANU (Tanzania). In both the countries, as also in Papua New Guinea, there exist various mobilisation structures linked to the political system: mass organisations of women and youth; workers' councils; people's councils and assemblies at various levels as part of the formal governmental machinery. Such organisations can serve a multitude of participatory and mobilising purposes and can exert pressure on governmental bureaucracies for intersectoral planning.

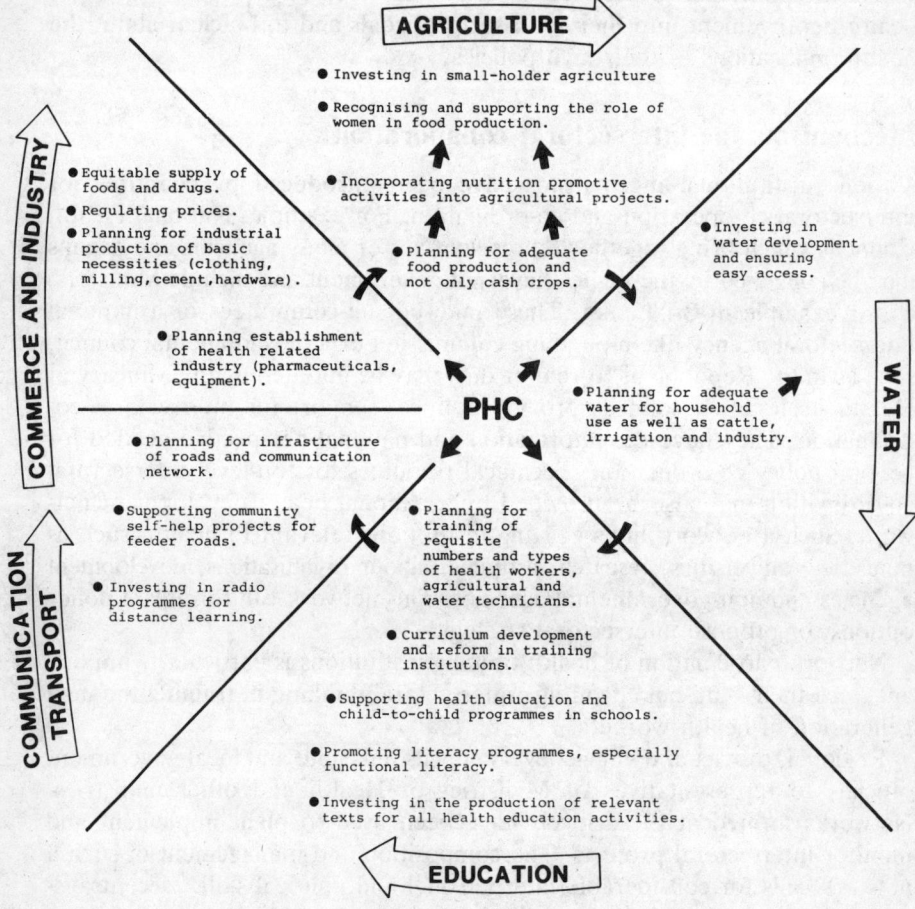

Fig. 9.1   Intersectoral collaboration for PHC

The communities' point of view

Communities tend to view the world in a holistic manner. On the other hand governments prefer division of labour and administrative fragmentation. No community's problems can be split into compartments labelled 'agriculture', 'education', 'health', 'labour' and so on. Such distinctions, required for administrative tidiness, leave different agencies in charge of different parts of community life. When this happens the linkages between different problems get obscured. Hence the need to challenge shallow sectoral definitions.

What are the main sectors relating to PHC?

The main sectors relating to PHC which will be outlined are agriculture and livestock, formal and non-formal education, community development, housing, water, sanitation and public works, information, industry and commerce, and the private sector (Fig. 9.1).

Agriculture and livestock sector

It is estimated that more than two-thirds of the people in developing countries derive their livelihood from agriculture. The well-being of most rural populations depends on their obtaining adequate income from their farms or from agricultural labour. They need energy for agricultural work. They also need protection from the health hazards of agricultural technology such as pesticides. Experience indicates that income from cash crops is usually controlled by men and may in fact be used to purchase consumer goods which do not include foods. Thus the nutritional status of children and other vulnerable groups suffers.

The contribution of women and children in farm work is important. In sub-Saharan Africa women are said to account for 30−50 per cent of all agricultural labour. Much of the existing stagnation in rural agriculture and its negative health consequences can be blamed on ignoring the special needs of women farmers.

Adverse health effects of agricultural production can occur where there is a change towards producing cash-crops instead of food for consumption. There may also be changes in benefits derived from new developments in agricultural methods. Introduction of modern technology can even by-pass large segments of the farming population including agricultural labour thus leading to further impoverishment. This has been the case in Mexico, Brazil and several countries of Latin America.

In many countries small-holders are the mainstay of agriculture, and also tend to be more efficient. Price incentives and adequate marketing of small-farm products are essential for agricultural development. In some countries production of cash crops has been given preferential treatment and so the feeding of the people has been left to the vagaries of international economic forces.

Livestock rearing occupies the major part of the time and energy of millions of people. Livestock provide food and drink, articles of clothing such as skins and hide products; power for ploughing, pumping water, grinding grain and transport. Livestock also provide fuel in the form of dung and organic manure. In some instances livestock also determine the location and movements of whole population groups such as nomadic pastoralists. In many communities livestock provide the basis for wealth and status as well as economic exchanges.

Livestock can process forage and waste crop materials inedible by man into nutritionally desirable food products, many of high protein, mineral and vitamin content and including some of high calorific value. Approximately 40 per cent of the total land available in developing countries can be used only for some form of forage production and a further 30 per cent is classified as forest with some potential for the production of forage. In addition, some 12 per cent of the world's total population live in areas where food crops cannot be easily grown and where people depend entirely on the products obtained from ruminant livestock.

Agricultural policy implications for PHC

In most countries policies and decisions relating to agricultural production are not related to health considerations. Health professionals generally have not developed the skills and information systems at local or national levels to advise their agricultural counterparts on the likely impact of different options on people's health.

The impact of health on agriculture, however, is better understood than the effect of agriculture on health. For example, the control of endemic diseases has often improved prospects for agricultural growth and created new potentials for development, such as the Onchocerciasis Control Programme in the Volta River Basin Area in West Africa. However, not enough is presently known about the adverse health risks in existing or planned agricultural processes and projects. Macro-agricultural policies and strategies need to be carefully analysed.

Policy on farm prices, taxes, producer subsidies and agricultural credit can all affect the crop mix and shifts in production and consumption away from health-damaging to health-promoting products.

A package of policies will also determine the purchasing power of vulnerable groups and their consumption level. Policies are needed to fulfil both the objectives of growth and equity: Peru recently announced a policy aimed at improving the nutritional status of the poor by shifting the emphasis from exports of fish meal to fertilise European crops to fish as food for local consumption.

During the past 15 years many countries have established national food and nutrition councils, often under a national planning authority. However, the effect of such councils is reported to have been limited. Further action is needed through having clearly defined policies and agendas for intersectoral action, as well as personnel who understand the intersectoral issues involved. In addition, researchers involved in health and nutrition have often been isolated in medical schools, and more cut off from the socio-economic aspects of nutrition than agricultural researchers.

In **Nepal** in the 1970s a National Nutrition Co-ordinating Committee was established. A national workshop was held which formulated the Pokhara Declaration for the Eradication of Malnutrition. The intersectoral national nutrition strategy included establishment of a nutrition section in the Health Ministry and nutrition focal points in the Ministries of Food and Agriculture, Education, Home and Panchayat.

Several countries have installed systems for nutritional surveillance which can provide a wealth of information for tracking the links between agriculture and health. The links between poverty and nutrition are complex. Some experiences indicate that income generating and nutrition improving activities can best be built up from below, around small groups whose members recognise each other as sharing similar situations.

For example, the Grameen Rural Bank for the Poor in **Bangladesh** offers short-term, small-scale and low cost credit to the landless. By the end of 1982, 24 000 group members, of whom over 9000 were female, had taken loans through 25 Bank Units reaching 428 villages. The range of activities funded was trading 29 per cent, livestock and fisheries 25 per cent, processing and manufacturing 20 per cent, services 16 per cent, shopkeeping 5 per cent, peddling 2.4 per cent, and agriculture and forestry 1.7 per cent. Female borrowers concentrated on livestock and fisheries (61 per cent).

Formal and non-formal education sectors

The education sector as a whole can be divided into 'formal' education as in primary and secondary schooling and further education, and non-formal education as in adult education and literacy programmes. The school system presents unique opportunities for forming and influencing children's health attitudes and behaviour during the formative periods of childhood and adolescence. Outside the school system, a wide variety of institutions and programmes are engaged in activities with an educational content, such as adult education programmes, religious institutions, literacy programmes, training and extension services, non-governmental organisations and the mass media. These may relate directly or indirectly to health.

The beneficial effects of the educational level of mothers on the health of families are well described in a number of studies and will not be discussed further. The education sector should therefore be of special interest for health planners. Intersectoral links need to be established for relevant curricula development, production of texts and for teacher training. Moreover the educational infrastructure, unlike the health infrastructure, extends to remote areas. In Kenya it was noted that one fifth of the population was going through primary schooling at any one time. It was suggested that with further training, teachers might well become better at providing promotive health care than are the existing health workers. Teachers are in close contact with their communities and can communicate freely. Often in remote communities the teacher may be the only knowledgeable person available for advice and help.

Teachers can be taught to recognise common diseases, physical, mental or emotional, and deal with or refer them. Besides teachers there is also another figure with great potential and significance for improving school and family health. That figure is the 'older child' in the family, often already caring for younger children and performing a range of household tasks such as water carrying and caring for livestock. Through a 'child-to-child' approach the older child can widen his/her health knowledge and skills for improvement of individual and family health. In this sense such children are 'agents of change'.

Health education for children in schools should be seen as having lifelong benefits.

> In **Panama** three different ministries guided by the Ministry of Health set up innovative schools in rural, relatively isolated areas. The curriculum was designed to be consistent with their normal community and family life-style and provide training and life experiences critical to farming and raising livestock, using modern techniques and new knowledge, and better systems of organisation and management. Local children learned the fundamentals of nutrition, basic health needs, water and irrigation, as well as reading, writing and arithmetic.

Adult education and community involvement

At the time of independence all countries inherited a large backlog of illiteracy. Since then the spread of literacy and schooling has been a major developmental goal for all nations. For cultural and other reasons illiteracy is more common amongst women. In south Asia female literacy is estimated at 31 per cent and in sub-Saharan Africa 34 per cent. In 1982 the average rate of primary school attendance for girls in developing countries (excluding India and China) was 58 per cent. In 16 countries it was below 50 per cent and in nine below 25 per cent.

All countries have established programmes for adult literacy with varying degrees of success. Such a process can become a forum for increasing awareness and a tool for community involvement. In South India, a progressive medical school has been involved in a rural health development project. At first the average literacy rate in the community was 33 per cent (male 53 per cent, female 18 per cent). In 1980—81, 30 centres were selected to cover 9000 people in an adult education programme for people aged 15—35 years. Time and meeting places were adapted to the learners' needs. Functional literacy was the main focus and a variety of innovative approaches like drama, film shows etc. were used to maintain interest. At evaluation 45 per cent of the participants had acquired facilities for poultry or dairy production, small businesses, self-employment or jobs in the private sector. As awareness and self-confidence increased 28 per cent had entered savings schemes and 25 per cent had put electricity into their homes. The adult education process like the one described above of mobilising and empowering people helps to create authentic community involvement which in many cases spreads to other sectors of development.

An ideal situation to work towards is one in which every adult education worker has the opportunity to acquire specific health knowledge and skills and every health worker has the opportunity to learn specific educational methods and skills. But perhaps the most potent contribution that adult education can make to PHC remains that of encouraging individuals as critical and creative beings who are capable of generating and acquiring knowledge and taking part in the kinds of social transformation which is necessary if the goals of PHC are to be achieved.

It is in this particular area that health workers and adult educators need to communicate more and to exchange experience, so that the effects of community involvement and mobilisation can be clearly understood. Sometimes mobilisation for PHC is confined largely to action for specific health purposes. In the last decade, however, mobilisation for PHC has come to imply mobilisation for social change as well, and often relates to agrarian reform or to the development of workers' organisations. These kinds of activities, which challenge the status quo, can and have produced effects of far-reaching consequence. In some places nation-wide political and socio-economic changes have resulted in the kinds of societies in which the goals of Health for All are being pursued vigorously. In other places, in the absence of nation-wide changes, PHC goals are being pursued on a smaller scale. In the latter case mobilisation and community involvement for PHC have not infrequently resulted in violent outcomes. It is not a coincidence that in the parts of the Americas at present torn by strife, an increasing number of community level promotors have been attacked. The social and political consequences of community mobilisation for PHC have yet to be fully assessed. Meanwhile, they continue to be promoted verbally and casually, almost on a par with improved sanitation and home gardens. There is therefore an urgent need for more awareness and responsibility in acknowledging the real effects of community mobilisation for PHC.

Community involvement in PHC has often been more successful where it was linked to intersectoral co-operation. In some instances community involvement started with PHC but moved on into other areas of development. In Tanzania, for example, experience of community diagnosis and control in a Tanzanian village led to community projects in productive and economic activities and in acquisition of clean drinking water. The incidence of schistosomiasis was reduced by 50 per cent in two years and the illiteracy rate dropped from 70 per cent to 50 per cent. The approach is being replicated all over Tanzania. In Chile, women's groups which developed increased self-confidence through a project, began demanding a greater say in local health activities. Women involved in nutrition clubs in Indonesia moved into developing an economic programme. Health committee members in Senegal became more interested in education. In some cases health programmes have evolved out of non-health experiences of community involvement, such as farmers' co-operatives in Venezuela or the post revolutionary experience of the National Literacy Crusade of Nicaragua which preceded health campaigns and programmes.

Community development and women's development

'Community development', in the 1950s, was the term used to describe the process by which people's participation was united with government development initiatives. Communities were assisted to identify their felt needs and to mobilise in self-help projects to improve their conditions and level of development. The term was then also applied to non-governmental development initiatives such as those connected with religious bodies, aid agencies, and workers' organisations. As the range of activities described under 'community development' broadened and multiplied other terms came into comon usage such as 'integrated development' and 'basic needs strategies'. This being so, many 'community development' activities have already been mentioned in this chapter, such as agricultural development or adult education initiatives. This section therefore will focus briefly on some key aspects of women's role in community development.

By 1972 a UN report noted that few countries had established comprehensive policies and strategies for nation-wide women's development. Rather, the process was an ad hoc one where women participated in general development programmes, assisted the sick and elderly, cared for children and were involved in educational, cultural and welfare programmes. There were few integrated programmes based on women's actual needs such as stressing the efficiency of household and resource management in conditions of scarcity, or acknowledging their normal role as principal food producers. Neither was there sufficient co-ordination among the various services implementing women's programmes.

At community level prevailing conditions continue to hamper progress. Social prejudices, the low status of women, lack of educational and technological training opportunities and discriminatory laws and practices all interact as major constraints to women's development. Also, the work which women perform is not usually counted as productive. Women's work is not

138

included in the estimate of Gross National Product as much of it is performed in or near the home and is of a subsistence nature. By contrast, all able-bodied men are generally enumerated as economically active, yet not infrequently their work output is less than that of women.

Given their pivotal role in family life and family health the effective involvement of women in intersectoral development is crucial. There are several examples of attempts being made by women themselves, often from the most exploited sections of society, to define their own priorities and to change their conditions of existence.

For example, in **South India** a group of ten village women from the 'untouchable' class established their own Rural Women's Social Education Centre. They had originally come together through a national literacy campaign in which they worked as literacy teachers. The main focus of their work had been on health education. Their activities have now come to include drought relief, encouragement of the use of local remedies, and participatory activities to raise the status of rural women.

Housing

Many houses in both developing rural and urban areas lack the minimum resources to provide adequate shelter. Housing of poor quality often fails to protect against heat, cold and wind and rain, disease-carrying insects and rodents and unhealthy air due to poor ventilation. House materials may be inflammable. Bad siting may expose residents to flooding, external noise and air pollution. Overcrowding can intensify health hazards.

In order to confront the interrelated problems outlined above co-ordinated action is required in many sectors. For example, prevailing policies and legislation will have to be adjusted relating to standards and location of housing, land availability, title and tenure. Even though slum and squatter upgrading programmes have become common, rarely is any health ministry or agency involved in their design or implementation, despite the programme's stated intention of improving health.

In Maputo in **Mozambique**, through community mobilisation and by enabling most of the urban dwellers to afford improved housing, slums have been transformed into healthier, cleaner neighbourhoods.

Water, sanitation and environment

Nearly one half of the population of developing countries suffers from health problems related to unsafe water and inadequate sanitation. In 1980

139

only 33 per cent of the rural and 74 per cent of the urban populations used sanitary disposal facilities, compared with 50 per cent in urban areas. Lack of safe and adequate water and facilities for the safe disposal of human faeces and solid wastes along with inadequate control of disease vectors and food safety, all combine as indicators of poverty and ill health.

At the same time, rapid industrialisation, disorderly urban expansion and the transformation of agriculture have brought about widespread use of chemicals, some of which are harmful. Current approaches in the development of water and sanitation tend to focus on the technical and engineering components and neglect the community's capacity and motivation for their use and maintenance. Water management projects are usually good 'entry points' for intersectoral co-operation between health, agriculture and environmental activities. However, experience shows that increased availability of safe water supplies does not in itself ensure increased access, utilisation and health improvements.

In the same country several agencies may often be found with some responsibility for water, including ministries of public works, hydraulics, health, agriculture, housing and regional administration. This fragmentation prevails also at the local level and perpetuates the status quo preventing the search for a coordinated approach.

A global survey conducted by WHO in 1983 revealed that 93 per cent of countries have three or more community water supply and sanitation agencies, 87 per cent have five or more and 35 per cent have nine or more. The survey also revealed that in several countries the intersectoral policy making body for health and the counterpart institutions for water and sanitation had no relationship.

Another factor which profoundly influences the environment in which humans and animals live and work is deforestation. The rural effects of this phenomenon are well known. The following example is an example of urban intersectoral co-operation.

In Visakhopatnam in **India** the municipality of the city (population: 0.8 million) runs a project for the rehabilitation of women and physically handicapped for 'social forestry'. Nineteen thousand plants have been set on road margins and wastelands. Women, leprosy-cured persons and physically handicapped have been selected to care for the plants. Each has about 100–200 plants and is given a site near the plants to erect a house and stall where tea/matches/cigarettes etc. are sold. The municipality pays two rupees a month for every surviving plant. Ninety people have been involved so far and the plant survival rate is 99 per cent.

Information and media

The use of radio for distance teaching in Tanzania and Botswana has been referred to in Chapter 3. The health sector still needs to appreciate the potential of the mass media for conveying health messages and influencing social behaviour. Traditional methods like minstrels, puppeteers, and roving theatre groups are also important in some countries. Almost half of the 600 000 villages in India enjoy the services of such groups on a regular basis. These entertainers have learnt the art of putting over messages in a simple language often using jokes. This has been used for spreading health information.

In **Nicaragua** communication for health and development is enhanced by the media. National campaigns are advertised extensively on radio and television and in the newspapers. Commercially prepared and locally constructed posters also advertise events as well as a newsprint booklet for public education, the 'folleta popular'. These are written at a basic level of education, incorporating humour and many drawings, to reinforce the content. They are designed through close and careful co-operation between adult educators and communication specialists.

Industry and commerce

The process of industrial growth is changing the living and working environment of a large number of people and giving rise to new health risks. National policies and strategies are needed to prevent the exploitation of poorer groups by industrial and commercial concerns. The siting of industries also requires careful planning in order to avoid an urban bias because of easy access to capital, market, raw materials and labour. Unplanned growth of industry has led to marked shifts of population with rapid growth of squatter areas in large cities.

In developed and some developing countries trade unions often serve to counterbalance the political pull of industry. They also serve as important means of protecting the health of workers in the work place and monitoring health risks of industrial occupation. The safeguarding of health in the work place is therefore closely associated with the political processes in a country and the role of trade unions and labour in the national system of decision making. Unfortunately in developing countries women workers and working children are at particular risk of multiple deprivations. Many informal sector activities are home based family enterprises, and outside of organised trade union activities. Hence new approaches must be developed for occupational health in the informal sector including that of agricultural labour.

Most developed countries and several developing ones have established systems for controlling and monitoring industrial pollution. The health sector needs to co-operate with other national agencies in monitoring the health impact and changing profile of health hazards caused by rapid technological change. In Singapore, the Ministry of Health established a unit of occupational health in 1968, which was later transferred to the Ministry of Labour and became the Division of Occupational Health. In 1970, a chair in occupational health was created within the department of Community Medicine at the National University and a training programme at the postgraduate level was started. At the same time dialogue between three major sectors of labour, economic planning and the University led to the development of a modern occupational health service in Singapore.

Many technological changes are also occurring in agriculture. In one major Asian country nearly 100 000 tonnes of pesticides are used each year and at least 70 per cent contain pesticides banned or severely restricted in industrial countries on safety grounds. In another developing country 50 per cent of food samples were found to be contaminated by pesticide residues and of these 30 per cent exceeded permissible limits. Hence a careful watch and protective legislation are needed.

In the Dominican Republic drugs and pesticides whose sale and use are restricted in the country of origin can only be marketed under the strict control of the State Secretariat for Public Health and Social Welfare and the State Secretariat for Agriculture.

Non-governmental and private sector

Many of the major health hazards in developed countries are already reaching significant proportions in the developing countries. These include unhealthy working conditions, unemployment, 'junk' food, smoking, alcoholism, environmental pollution and traffic accidents. Co-operation between the health sector and a wide range of governmental and non-governmental agencies is thus required.

Within the private health sector are modern health practitioners and institutions and traditional ones, such as the Ayurvedic practitioners of India and the variety of local practitioners and healers in most developing rural areas. There are many examples of initiatives designed to include traditional health practitioners in primary health care activities. Perhaps the most well documented are those involving traditional birth attendants. Almost all developing countries now have training programmes for traditional birth attendants so that midwifery practices are undergoing a process of modernisation.

Building on experience: guidelines for future action

This section draws out some of the key issues of the chapter which can be used as guidelines for the further development of intersectoral co-operation.

National level policies and strategies
1. The health sector must come out of its relative isolation and collaborate with other sectors. Health goals and criteria need to be incorporated into policies and programmes of other sectors.
2. The health sector needs to assist other sectors in monitoring and evaluating

the health impact of development projects. This way negative health effects are anticipated and countered.

3. High priority should be given in development policies and plans to the special needs of vulnerable population groups. Such groups are at greatest risk of ill health. For geographical, political, social or financial reasons they are least able to take the initiative in seeking health care. Women, children, and the poorest industrial worker families comprise the vulnerable groups. The health sector needs to identify the vulnerable groups and the conditions of risk in which they live.

4. When governments adopt adjustment policies in times of economic crisis, such as in the recent widespread economic recession, the social cost of such adjustments needs to be foreseen. Nationally accepted criteria are needed to guide macro-economic policies to ensure that essential health needs of the population are satisfied.

5. Policy formulation, planning and legislation need to become part of the broader reorientation needed for intersectoral co-operation. To that effect restructuring of development policies at the national level may be needed.

6. Institutional and administrative reforms are required to co-ordinate the present sectoral and vertical programmes, create administrative structures and establish horizontal linkages between sectors.

7. Mechanisms need to be established in the form of national health councils, national health development networks, food and agricultural boards and so on. Such bodies may have representatives from ministries, political parties, trade unions, as well as from women's and youth organisations. Sub-committees and working groups set up by these national level councils can study specific technical subjects and help in formulating collaborative strategies.

The following case study from **Sri Lanka** will illustrate how a National Health Council (NHC) operates. The NHC in Sri Lanka was established in October 1980, chaired by the Prime Minister with the Minister of Health as the Convenor. The membership included 11 other Ministers. The mechanism for technical support for the top level NHC is the National Health Development Council (NHDC) consisting of secretaries of all the Ministries represented in the NHC, the secretary of the Ministry of Higher Education, the directors or their deputies from the various branches of the health service and representatives of WHO and UNICEF as observers. The major function of the NHDC has been to assure intersectoral co-ordination for the implementation of policy decisions taken by the NHC. Several standing committees may be called upon to help provide the technical inputs.

Intermediate level mechanisms and approaches
These levels include provincial and district level. It is sometimes easier in

practice to achieve intersectoral co-ordination at these levels even where there has not been higher level decision-making. This is also the case where decentralisation of government to provincial level has occurred. In both cases greater flexibility may exist to make intersectoral co-operation possible, often on a small scale or where it involves sharing limited resources.

1. Mechanisms for intersectoral co-ordination need to be established at these levels to explore possibilities for policy making, planning, implementation and monitoring of joint ventures. Provincial and district level councils or committees of various kinds need to be linked closely to the prevailing administrative/political structure.
2. In order to give orientation and brief training to the manpower in various sectors at intermediate level, short workshops have been found useful. Jointly planned, organised and evaluated, such workshops can form the base from which specific provincial and district level needs, potentials, problems, plans and actions can emerge.
3. During or following such a workshop the collection of baseline data using rapid survey techniques can provide a foundation on which sectoral workers and communities can build future development activities.
4. A 'core curriculum' for training intersectoral workers needs to be identified. This needs to take into consideration the different conceptual frameworks, methods and terminologies used by the various sectors. District and community level needs should determine what should be learnt and what types of co-operation are necessary between the various sectors at intermediate level.
5. Co-operation between sectors can be encouraged when special funds are made available for joint projects.

Community level
1. At community level communities themselves see their lives and activities as 'integrated' and not divided into separate 'sectors' for the convenience of government departments or agencies.
    Changes in one aspect of community life often affect all other aspects of community life, particularly where survival margins are minimal.
2. Damage can and has been done to community lifestyle and patterns of survival where there is little or no co-operation between sectors at community level. Such a 'fragmented' development approach usually fails to achieve its full potential, and will be wasteful of community time and energy.
3. It makes sense to commence with those intersectoral activities which have realistic and achievable goals. Experience of success and the confidence thereby gained can encourage those concerned for further action.
4. Health is not usually an expressed need. People's priority concerns are more with food, water, jobs and security. The health sector will have to be content with a back seat role in a number of developmental programmes so long as the goals fall within the defined activities of PHC.

5. Multiplier effects should be a priority for initial intersectoral projects.
6. The main role of experts is to help communities analyse their situation and provide advice and assistance without undermining self-reliance.
7. The effects of unco-ordinated action are felt most keenly by fieldworkers. It is they who have to deal directly with the communities, and their training should prepare them to work across sectoral boundaries.
8. At community level intersectoral co-operation should assist communities to create and manage their own participatory organisational structures. They then identify and relate to other groups, organisations and agencies through 'networking', and make field visits to similar projects.

Communities also need to learn to deal with the problems such as reduction or withdrawal of funds, periods when motivation is low, handling success and failure, and creating mechanisms for ongoing monitoring and evaluation of their own experiences and activities. In this way people themselves are put at the centre of their own development. This is one of the key objectives of intersectoral co-operation.

Further reading

Feuerstein, M.T., Lovell, H.J., Shaw, A.P.M., Editorial: 'Livestock and community development', Special issue, *Community Development Journal*, 1987.
Feuerstein, M.T., 'Mobilisation for Primary Health Care, Role of adult education, *Convergence*, 15:2 (Issue on Adult Education and Primary Health Care), published by ICAE, Toronto, 1982.
Food and Agricultural Organisation, *Evaluation of the Training of Fieldworkers through a Training Pack on Field Programme Management, Food and Nutrition*, Results from Chile, Burkina Faso and Philippines, Rome, F.A.O. 1986 (mimeo).
Lovel, H., Feuerstein, M.T., Editorial: 'Women, poverty and community development', *Community Development Journal*, 20:3, 1985.
United Nations Educational Social and Cultural Organisation, *Recommendations on the Development of Adult Education*, Paris, UNESCO, 1976.
World Health Organisation, *Intersectoral Action for Health*, Background Document for the Technical Discussions, Thirty-Ninth World Health Assembly, A39/Technical Discussions/1, Geneva, WHO, 1986.
World Health Organisation, *Strengthening Ministries of Health for Primary Health Care*, Offset Publication 82, Geneva, WHO, 1984.
World Health Organisation, *Report of the Technical Discussion of the Role of Intersectoral Cooperation in National Strategies for Health for All*, A39/Technical Discussions/4, Geneva, WHO, 1986.
International Council for Adult Education, *Our Own Health: The Role of Adult Education and Community Involvement in Primary Health Care*, Toronto, ICAE, 1984.

CHAPTER 10
NGOs and International Organisations

'NGOs are many and diverse. Their scale may be large, medium or small. Their support may come from external sources, from their own fund-raising, from government subventions, or from all these sources at once. Their principal activity may be direct service to those in need in the community, health education, or research, whether in the field or the laboratory; it may include a good deal of advocacy for changes in government policy. Their scene of activity may be confined mainly to urban areas or may deliberately be directed at underserved rural communities. Their attitude to government health policies may be supportive, neutral, occasionally even confrontational. Their concentration may be on establishing and maintaining institutions, or on caring for those suffering from a specific disease or disability and on attacking its causes with a view to prevention. They may have a real concern for the general health of the community but vary in their interpretation of the main priority: specific diseases? pure water supply? sanitation? mother and child care? road safety? nutrition? general health education? Their focus of action may accordingly be mothers, children, environmental planners, the education system of the community at large. They include full-time professionals and part-time volunteers, some with thorough training, others with none at all. Their motivation may be religious or compassionate. It may even be political or occasionally nothing better than self-promotion.'
WHO, Background paper at 38th World Health Assembly, May 1985

Whilst NGOs have had a long history of involvement in health and social issues, we are here only interested in the development of their role since the Second World War. They have often been the first to offer services or support for the poorest in many societies, and in this support, health care has always featured prominently. With respect to their role in primary

146

health care, there are two areas of interest:
- how NGOs have initiated and supported change;
- which groups are represented by the NGOs.

Initiating and supporting change

The work of NGOs often reflects shifts in public opinion, and, in turn, they have considerable effect on that public opinion. As a result, governments and societies have often changed in order to modify the conditions in question. The positive side of such influence is that more and more people have come to benefit from improved services, management and supportive legislation. The negative side is that deep and fundamental problems remain for these agencies to have an impact on the poorest sectors of any population.

As one of the major international organisations, UNICEF has played a prominent role in bringing the attention of governments to the needs of children − especially in disadvantaged situations. It was first set up to promote the health and welfare of the large numbers of families and children made destitute in Europe by the destruction caused in the Second World War. When it became obvious that problems for the welfare of children also existed in many Third World countries, UNICEF expanded its activities on a global scale. At first, it concentrated on the provision of supplies − food supplements, vaccines, equipment for health facilities and vehicles. It then turned to the support of primary health care, and, with WHO, convened an international conference at Alma-Ata in Russia in 1978 to establish general agreements on a definition of primary health care, and the elements of that care that should receive attention. More recently, it has entered the field of active health assistance − most notably in the promotion of the use of a few simple technologies under its programme of GOBI-FFF (Growth monitoring, Oral rehydration, Breast feeding, Immunisation, Family planning, Female education and Food supplementation).

The World Health Organisation has followed a similar development, although this has always been more in 'technical' areas − assisting countries to build up their health service systems. WHO played a very important part in co-ordinating the effort to eradicate smallpox and yaws. At present, it has considerable concern with the issues of management in primary health care, and has developed programmes for Expanded Immunisation, and Control of Diarrhoeal Diseases.

The efforts of these organisations to secure international agreement on the future strategies for health improvement led to a definition at Alma-Ata of primary health care. This definition (often referred to as Primary Health Care) was very important in that it focussed international attention on the failures of existing health service systems to deal adequately with the health problems of those who suffered most ill health. However, because the definition had to be arrived at through a process of compromise to allow for different political ideologies, and because it had to be based on the existing

147

links and support offered by the agencies, the final definition remained very health service oriented, and crucially ambiguous on the nature of the political process necessary for health. The ambiguity was between
- PHC as a complex of health-related *services* in which people participate, and whose advice people should follow; and
- PHC as a form of *social support*, involving the inputs of all members of society (including *all* services), that results in improved health.

This ambiguity can be seen in the present argument between those who advocate a technological 'fix' for ill health (selective PHC) and those who see the improvement of health as the result of a complex societal process (comprehensive PHC). More importantly, the ambiguity has allowed NGOs to follow several different paths in their search for methods of improving health. This diversity has shown us the variety of possible end points, all of which have their own peculiar validity. Thus, there is no doubt that technological fixes can be beneficial to a lot of people. The difficulties arise when one examines the plight of those who cannot benefit from these fixes. Equally, social change may be possible to a degree, but there seem to be several limitations and possible interpretations of the notion of equity: one simple example is the assessment of extent to which society is responsible for an individual.

International NGOs, such as Oxfam, Save the Children Fund, and Christian Aid, have had a distinctive record in supporting local efforts in these various interpretations and difficulties. Not being encumbered with ideological or policy requirements, their value lies in their being able to test models of social and service action, in addition to providing welcome support.

A good example is that of Jamkhed in **India**, as has been described in Chapter 2 (page 13). The project, in the initial stages, received assistance from Christian Aid and Oxfam to commence a comprehensive health programme. After starting with the provision of curative and preventive services at a local clinic, which earned credibility, the project later developed into a more comprehensive and community based activity. It is quite possible to maintain that without the services the project would have got nowhere, and would have ended up by providing nothing.

Simavi, an organisation in the Netherlands, has been involved in a programme of integrated rural development in Tanzania for nine years since 1976. This was based at the district level, and therefore gave a realistic picture of the problems encountered and the managerial as well as material inputs required. It also provided good experience of the administrative, political and social groundwork needed for sustained development. The experience taught many lessons with regard to the training and support of front line health workers. There are several such examples where NGO-sponsored projects have helped to break new ground and experiment with new models of care. The distillation of such experience, coupled with the efforts of some governments and individual workers, helped to create the present international focus on PHC, and provides its validation through experience.

These and many similar examples, demonstrate that PHC projects, at international and local levels, often have to get off the ground through a process of political compromise. There is also a growing acceptance that *everyone* has a say in health, no matter what their status in society. It is also obvious that diversity of approach can be beneficial, rather than merely chaotic.

NGOs as representatives

Probably the most important factors determining health in any community are the resources and social support available to a family. The types of intervention necessary for health will therefore differ according to the family. Families with sufficient resources and support merely require a health service that will provide them with treatment, preventive measures, and advice that they can follow using the resources and support they have. However, the people who suffer most from ill health and early death (and who contribute most to the poor health statistics in many countries) do not have such resources or support. They belong to the weakest, poorest, least powerful, least supported, most isolated, and most vulnerable families in any community. This is true whether the community is rural or urban, whether it is in a well-served or poorly-served area, whether it is in a rich country or poor country. From the point of view of such families, whoever truly represents their interests, whoever contributes positively to an environment in which they can achieve self-respect, and self-reliance will therefore have the more significant impact on their health.

The potential of any organisation serving communities (whether or not governmental) will vary according to the particular type of organisation it is, and according to which people it represents. In this respect, it is not fair to talk in general terms of whether governments are better or worse than other organisations: they offer different types of representation. In some respects, NGOs will be more relevant in certain aspects of PHC and in others governments will be better.

For raising protest about local problems, rapid response to local need, clear outlining of local situations, personal concern over the fate of local people, and ability to change plans or programmes in the light of the local situation, it would be hard to better some NGOs − notably those created by the communities themselves. This is because the NGOs most representative of communities *as a whole* are those created by community members. Such organisations, created in order to preserve health and support *everyone* in a community, go back as far as we know. However, such movements have recently had to become more complex as the gap between rich and poor has increased in societies, and traditional societal structures have broken down. Perhaps the nearest to this type of non-governmental organisation nowadays is represented by individuals who have left a community for further education, and later return to it to provide leadership in the changes necessary for all to maintain good health.

One step up from this is the type of NGO that sends staff to work in particular areas for long periods of time. In this way, they can become familiar with local politics and needs, and gradually become more relevant to the problems of the different groups of families. In some countries, priests may provide a good example of this type of involvement. Inevitably, though, the views of such staff will be coloured by the views of the organisation they represent, and it is only in very rare cases that they can justifiably claim to represent the community in a totally non-partisan way.

A step further away from this is achieved by the organisation that maintains a permanent presence (in the form of a health centre or clinic, for example) but can only maintain staff there for short periods of time (up to five years or so).

Finally, there are the remotest NGOs of all — those who provide funds and/or advice from afar. Their base can be in the capital of the country concerned or even in a different country.

Agencies which work closely over extended periods of time *within* communities, are more likely to be aware of the needs of the most deprived groups. The further away from the people the agency is, the more difficult this becomes.

The impact of PHC on NGOs

Often, those who have been influenced least by the current PHC movement are the NGOs built by communities themselves: they were already fully involved in PHC in the sense that they were catering for the health of all through a system of societal support. The organisations for which adaptation has been more problematic are those which are more remote.

The remote NGOs

As has been suggested, the remote NGOs have tried to adapt themselves in different ways. Most do this on the basis of what they understand by PHC and in the light of what they consider as priorities. The diversity of NGOs also plays a significant part. Many have a strong religious element on which they depend for fund-raising and volunteers. In the constitutions of many NGOs, provision of services and charity play key roles. Again, whilst some NGOs see their aim as an extension of basic health services, others see it as a way to mobilise the community as an equal partner in the process of health development.

On the whole, the NGOs previously working in general community development have taken the more 'equity-conscious' of the interpretations of the PHC definition, whereas the major health-service NGOs have tended to opt for the 'service provision' interpretation. The word 'equity' in this context applies as much to the relation between services, and the relation between services and the people, as it does to the relation between classes of people.

The choice of a 'service' interpretation has led to some interesting dilemmas for the health-service NGOs. 'Contact', the organ of the Christian Medical Commission (CMC) published the following comment from a group of CMC commissioners in 1985 in an issue titled 'Setting our Priorities for Health': 'As PHC and HFA programmes are implemented, it remains likely that the poorest and most powerless, even in poor communities, will not be reached. The CMC, with its commitment to serving the poor, could give special emphases to these people, including considering how to define and reach the poor and how to assess the impact of programmes on their health and development status.'

Contact went on to describe how 'The hard discussions on this priority, therefore, centred not on the concept of PHC, but on what directions really helpful and innovative approaches to PHC should be taking'. As a result, the CMC thought that two ways to 'expand and extend the benefit of PHC' were to:

1. Study and talk about successful examples of PHC integrating with established health services, and describe how the various health sectors can complement one another.
2. Study ways and means of increasing the impact of PHC by increasing the numbers of people involved. 'It is not that small programmes are not good, but with so many more to be touched by even the most basic health services, how can we begin to reach out to them faster?'

These statements are noteworthy in several respects. They assume:

1. PHC programmes can be run without affecting the poorest.
2. The poor are treated as 'service recipients'.
3. The concept of PHC is not to be brought into question.
4. 'Expanding and extending PHC' involves principally the health services.
5. 'Reaching out' should be done by more people.

On the basis of the 'service' interpretation of PHC, such assumptions are, of course, correct: the Alma-Ata declaration allows them as a valid base from which to approach PHC. This interpretation naturally leads to the development of 'extended service providers' such as village health workers, primary health workers, trained traditional birth attendants, and to co-operation with other health service providers such as traditional healers and government health services. Very many health service (and some non-health service) NGOs have thus embarked on PHC programmes that involve all of the above developments: their management and training structures have been adapted accordingly.

Even though this approach may well leave out the poorest in many ways, the achievements that can be made using this approach must not be under-estimated. There is no doubt that several programmes have brought about a reduction in morbidity and mortality using such an approach. This is especially so when the remaining PHC 'service' elements (water, education, sanitation and so on) have been brought in for the community to be served.

Furthermore, many local NGOs have used such a service approach as a stepping stone to the other, 'equity' approach.

There are several reasons why so many service NGOs seem to prefer this approach. One of the reasons is that it is relatively easy, in management terms, to incorporate into existing frameworks. It is, after all, merely an extension of an existing approach.

Local NGOs

It is interesting to note that the key element linking many projects based at local level is broad representation of all groups of families in a community. For local people, speaking the native language as a mother tongue, this is relatively easy to achieve, though requiring many years of work. For more remote NGOs, the only way in is to be ready to learn from local people, learn from mistakes, and avoid the imposition of any programme that is anything but straightforwardly service in nature. A programme that has tried such a cautious approach is the one mounted by the Private Hospital Association of Malawi. This is an NGO that represents all the mission health facilities, and several non-mission health units, in Malawi. In 1982, following a pilot project initiated by the government, PHAM held a meeting for all its members at which it was decided that the members would like to join forces in establishing a common approach to PHC that could be integrated with the government approach. They elected a co-ordinator to work from the PHAM headquarters, who also became a member of the national team that was responsible for training and policy in PHC. It was decided quite quickly that the approach used in the pilot project (a rather 'traditional' one, using village health committees and village health workers), was not viable, and so a new approach was gradually developed.

Initially, this was based much more on the 'equity' definition referred to above, but it was found that service personnel, from whatever service sector they were chosen, were unable to approach the communities on an equal basis. This was partly because their individual sectors (health included) had rigid vertical programmes that each ministry insisted on being accomplished. As a result, the exploratory, open-ended, problem-solving approach that they were taught was left unused. It had been hoped that if service personnel used such an approach, they would better understand problems within com-munities, would realise that the poorest were the ones benefitting least from their efforts, and would work as a team towards becoming more relevant to the poorest. Unfortunately, the conflicts with policy were too great — none of the national policies could be seen as 'equity based' in any sense.

Therefore, a modified, and perhaps more realistic approach was tried that emphasised the necessity of *including* all members of a community in current service efforts. This meant agreeing that services as provided were relevant and useful for a large section of the population (those who had the resources and support necessary to benefit from the services and their advice). As such, they should continue unmodified. However, it was equally necessary to provide a different type of service for those who could not benefit from the services.

In PHAM, this meant establishing a very simple approach based on the perceptions and problems of health workers. They were helped to approach a community and describe the problems as *they* saw them, and try to achieve agreement about the causes of those problems. Was the health worker doing something wrong? Were some people unable to follow advice? Had people tried advice and failed? Were there social barriers to participation? It was through this approach that workers could modify their services so that the poorest could cope with the most common health problems *as seen at the clinic* (diarrhoea, malaria, and pneumonia were those most often found in many areas). In addition, PHAM ensured the availability of scales for growth monitoring in villages near the trained health units so that mothers could weigh their own children if they wished to. Complex messages about oral rehydration with salts or about nutrition were largely dropped until every person in a village could understand and cope with the illnesses focussed on. This approach was well appreciated by ordinary people, and at least ensured total coverage. In addition, relationships between staff and people much improved. Unfortunately, it has almost nothing to do with equity in a political sense, and the policies in Malawi will be unlikely to change as a result of this programme. The only hope is that, as more service personnel come to grapple with the problems of the poor as a result of the programme, some of the realities will percolate back to the policy-makers.

The difference of this programme from the one at Jamkhed (and perhaps its greatest weakness) is that it was set up by people and organisations remote from the communities they had to deal with. True representation of the poor could not be achieved, and only advocacy to those who did represent communities could be tried.

There are many examples of programmes that have tried the 'traditional' primary health worker model, but have not gone on to modify it. It is this group that presents the most danger to the 'Primary Health Care Movement' since the protagonists of such schemes firmly believe that their concept is right, and that the lack of total impact or coverage is a result of poor methodology *within* the concept – rather than as a result of the particular interpretation of PHC that they are using. In this way NGOs can come across intractable dilemmas – as the quote from the CMC magazine shows.

Of course it is true that the methodology may leave much to be desired. There are countless instances of PHC projects being set up in this service context by excited individuals, and large numbers of volunteers being trained in basic curative and preventive health services. It is true that such projects often fail after only a short time (in terms of impact on health) because few people apply the same health service logic to such situations as they would in normal health services. Simple concepts such as coverage, exclusive focus on priorities, and measurement of real impact amongst the families with the most suffering are often left aside. Instead, activities such as the number of mothers trained, the numbers of latrines built, the numbers of patients seen, or the number of meetings held with 'communities' are often held up as signs of progress.

However, to criticise such projects on this basis would be to miss the important point that it is not just the methodology at issue. It is vitally important that any NGO, whether a funding agency, or a service agency, or one working within a community, states clearly which concept of PHC it aims to support, and how it hopes to achieve it. Once this is clear, then the management issues for that programme can be sorted out.

The implications from the examples given above are that:

1. It becomes more difficult for NGOs to be truly representative the further they are from communities. This inevitably leads them to a greater service orientation and the 'service' approach to PHC. The service approach will tend to favour those with adequate resources and support, and so must lead to a compromise in the efficacy of the service for the poorest.

2. If a service approach is chosen, then the criteria for the usefulness of such a service must be equally applied at every level of the service.

3. If an 'equity' approach is chosen, then the critical factor is the training of the staff running the service. It becomes irrelevant whether primary health workers are used or not. The staff have to have a radically different interpretation of their roles with regard to the society they serve, and they must be exploratory, problem-oriented and open to suggestion from the people they serve about how to tackle problems. This is very difficult for a remote NGO to achieve, as it requires a great deal of time and effort in retraining and supporting staff.

The contribution of NGOs to country health programmes

It is well known that the efforts of many NGOs, governments, and individual workers led to the concern of the international agencies with PHC. But this experience came piecemeal. Before the Second World War, most of the major NGOs had an overtly religious bias. Mission hospitals had been established in almost all developing countries. In many countries of sub-Saharan Africa, up to a third of all hospital services are still provided by voluntary agency hospitals. In India, there are more than 200 such hospitals, and several medical schools which have acquired international reputation. Their experiences have contributed much to the current PHC debate, especially since most mission hospitals are established in remote areas and therefore able to report and absorb experiences locally.

Again, their main ethos is that of service. They are often involved in activities which may be considered unpleasant by more elitist institutions, or by the society itself. Care of leprosy patients, for example, has been the

contact

Christian Medical Commission   World Council of Churches
150, route de Ferney   1211 Geneva 20   Switzerland

Number **68**

JUNE 1982

UNDERSTANDING THE CAUSES OF WORLD HUNGER

Fig. 10.1   The churches have had a long history of involvement with societal issues related to health

domain of missionary institutions in many countries. Now that care of leprosy patients and the disabled in general is becoming more community based, mission organisations again often take the lead, and have had much impact on international thinking. Care of the urban poor and street children has been the special domain of NGOs for over 200 years. Thus, the very ethos of NGOs often draws them to the heart of current problems. There is thus a definite need to create national structures through which their experience may be put to wider use. Many countries have taken a step towards this by absorbing the voluntary hospitals into the national service, even though this has sometimes meant a burdensome bureaucracy that can stifle initiative (Fig. 10.1).

The impact of NGOs internationally

The power of NGOs internationally has been demonstrated by a number of recent events. Whatever the views about such public events as Band-Aid and Sport-Aid, they certainly achieved some form of short-term international focus on crises in developing countries. It was, of course, inevitable that the focus was moved away from the disparities of the international economic order that created those problems in the first place.

Over a longer term, several international NGOs, such as Oxfam, War on Want and Christian Aid have successfully campaigned in the fields of breast

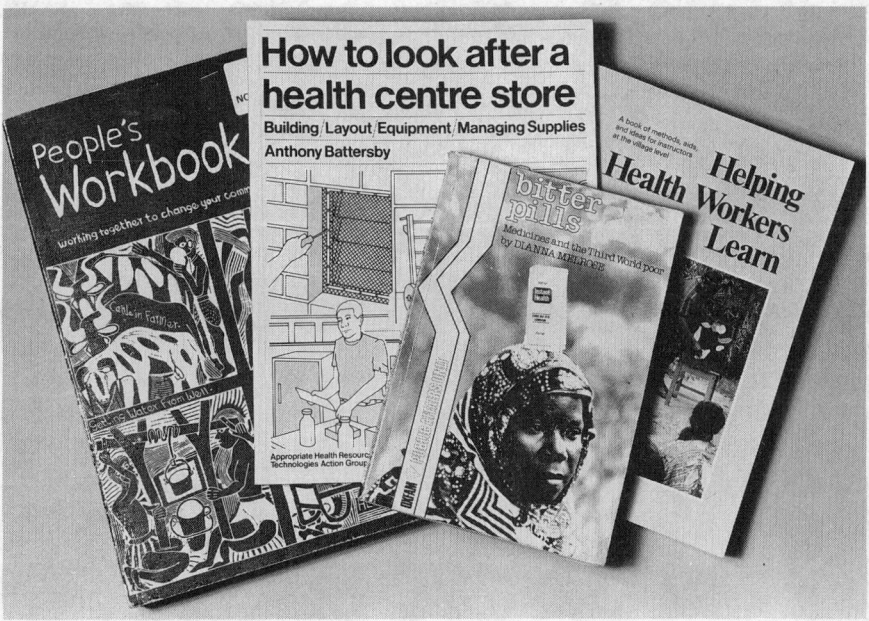

Fig. 10.2 NGOs have made important contributions in publishing, training, campaigns and promotional material

feeding, formula feeding, drug marketing, chemical dumping and legal reform. These successes have been made possible as a result of the shifts in public opinion, and more professional marketing and communication strategies by the media and the aid agencies.

The NGOs are also changing in their own outlook. In addition to the support of small-scale projects, more NGOs are developing their advocacy for shifts in international policy (Fig. 10.2). In future years, the debt crisis, disarmament and favourable terms of trade are likely to become major campaign issues for NGOs.

Countries also change. Developing countries cannot be put into one basket. Several have much capital and self-sufficiency in manpower, expertise, and resources. In some, growing levels of discontent in the middle classes, and increasing numbers of people with some form of education have led to moderation of dictatorship. Some countries, especially in sub-Saharan Africa, have had to face recurrent natural and man-made crises. NGOs, especially the churches, have had an important role in such situations. They can often bring a fresh look to problems. They can contribute to the analysis of interacting trends and help in the emergence of a composite solution. This is where some of the international institutions are at their weakest, because of their narrow outlooks. When international organisations can learn to join hands with their local counterparts to evolve local solutions, there may be scope for greater and better support of PHC. As has been shown, NGOs often have the important advantage of nearness to problems through resident representatives and workers, or are constituted of such local people. They have a less cumbersome mechanism for policy making and responding to emergencies. However, they can equally be the reactionary and conservative forces against change – sometimes preserving a narrow-minded and hostile outlook on anything that might challenge their secure form of life. In either case, they are always a powerful voice that demands listening to.

Further reading

Walt, G. and Vaughan, P., *Development of the Primary Health Care Approach*, London, Ross Institute, 1981.

World Health Organisation, *Collaborating with Non-Governmental Organisations in Implementing the Global Strategy for Health For All*, Background document for the Technical Discussions at the 38th World Health Assembly, 10–11 May 1985, A38/Technical Discussions/1, Geneva, World Health Organisation, (Mimeo).

Chambers, R., *Rural Development – Putting the Last First*, London, Longman, 1983.

'Setting our Priorities for Health', *CONTACT*, publication of the Christian Medical Commission, No. 58, June 1985.

CHAPTER 11
Challenges for the Future

The 1980s represent the first half of the target period leading up to Health for All by 2000. In the ten years since the Alma-Ata Declaration a great deal has happened. The Declaration helped to focus thought internationally, in government departments and ministries as well as in academic circles on the important issue of PHC. Encouraged and led by the international agencies like the World Health Organisation (WHO) and UN Children's Fund (UNICEF) the foundations of much of the conceptual framework of PHC have been laid. At the time of Alma-Ata several countries like China, Cuba and Sri Lanka were already on the way to achieving PHC. A great deal of their experience helped to define PHC and came to be carefully analysed. In sub-Saharan Africa a number of poor countries like Tanzania and Zambia had taken brave decisions challenging the established dogma and had diverted scarce resources into grass-roots health development. These experiences helped to demonstrate that even poor countries can improve their standards of health. At Alma-Ata the eight elements of PHC were defined. But more importantly the issues of equity, social justice and community participation were given as much importance as that of health coverage. They came to be recognised as the purpose as well as the outcome of universal health coverage. Each one of the countries mentioned above has progressed towards PHC by a different route. There is no single approach. PHC is both a concept and a process.

Every nation must evolve its own path to PHC based on its political, social and cultural heritage. The building blocks of PHC may not be dissimilar, for example the use of auxiliaries, community health workers, trained birth attendants, traditional healers etc. It is up to the country to use what building blocks can be made most readily available. China used bare-foot doctors. Tanzania and Zambia based their services on medical auxiliaries and are now commencing programmes of training village health workers. Cuba based her strategy entirely on physicians and other professionals. The second important development of the 1980s has been the growth of training material for the various cadres operating the PHC network. The emergence of local training material breaks the dependency on texts produced in the more affluent countries, and addresses a totally different set of priorities.

A sense of urgency with targets-related planning has been generated by Alma-Ata, for example Health For All by 2000; universal water and sanitation as well as immunisation for all by 1990, and so on. This has removed the complacency in health planning. Certain health issues cannot wait until tomorrow because of their potential for permanent damage to the human capital. This recognition has led to a drive for health improvement within the forseeable future. The wind of change internationally, together with a national will accompanied by the demands for better health by the people means that the focus of health planning must change rapidly.

Avoiding the pitfalls

Fundamental change in health planning and management poses a formidable outlook for Ministries of Health and related institutions. Activists may seize the opportunity to instigate change. But mindless change for its own sake can be dangerous as well as wasteful. What is needed are mechanisms for critical evaluation and review of the policies of the past, and their failures as well as successess. This can then provide a springboard for change.

A second pitfall is that PHC may become just another vertical programme with the bulk of health functioning continuing as before. Administrative convenience is not always the best answer, and shying away from fundamental change in health planning will only put off the day for facing the issues in organisational change, resource reallocation, health manpower development and so on. Country experiences described in this book provide illustrations of how these changes have been made in a variety of situations. Change does not necessarily happen through directives from above, even though the support of those in power is important. What is needed is to create the climate for change. The importance of 'committed individuals' developing larger groups and networks across the board, within and between ministries and with academic and other institutions cannot be overlooked. Such a network can be the firm foundation for progression towards PHC. It can also provide an intellectual forum for exchange of ideas. In the final run skills and techniques will be needed for managing change including those of compromise and conflict resolution. Using the appropriate approach change is possible even in the most firmly established institutions. In Britain, highly prestigious London medical schools have shared resources through a process of rationalisation. The process is continuing with the shift of resources to community services. Similarly some medical schools in developing countries have made significant changes in the curriculum to face the implications of PHC.

There can be pitfalls in opting for *selective* in contrast to *comprehensive* Primary Health Care. The difference is subtle and the pressures for quick results may be great. But selective PHC can trap countries into a cul-de-sac, whereas comprehensive PHC opens up a whole new vista of creative activity. Innovative medical technologies (for example, oral rehydration therapy) and development in scientific knowledge (for example, the importance of energy density of food rather than of protein) together with the national drive for immunisation create the opportunity for controlling several killer diseases. Access to mass media for national campaigns and for writing slogans, may be a means of involving high level politicians. Besides, statistics can be made readily available and results are quick and demonstrable. But selective PHC can overlook the vital issues of community participation and creation of health awareness. It may deflect efforts away from the task of building up and evolving a health infrastructure. Selective PHC can emphasise health delivery by know-all specialists at the expense of achievements by the people. The carrot of selective PHC with its promise of quick results may turn out to be risky in the long run. How countries will opt is difficult to predict. Sufficient momentum has been generated internationally for pursuing the goal of comprehensive PHC, and a few distractions may come to be ignored. Some political leaders may grab the opportunity of selective PHC to win popular support. The chances are that most countries will take the pragmatic approach of moving towards comprehensive PHC, in the meantime clearing the backlog through crucial national programmes like those for oral rehydration and immunisation, thereby obtaining the best of both approaches.

The management of change

The manner in which change is introduced is likely to prove decisive. In the examples given in this book we have seen many techniques for introducing change being put into practice. Bringing about any significant organisational change to support PHC can require the consent of large numbers of people. This entails a process of discussion, challenging existing ideas and ways of doing things. It also calls for redefinition of objectives and of translating them into action. We have seen that this is harder to do in some situations (for example hospitals) than others. It requires courage and commitment on the part of those in positions of responsibility and influence. But we have seen throughout the chapters of this book how a committed and wise leadership which works closely with the people involved can make improvements in the most difficult situations. In large national health systems, as we have seen in the chapters on Ministries of Health and District Management it requires systematic planning on long timescales and close co-ordination between different parts of the health system. An open style of management is required which frees channels of communication and welcomes constructive criticism. Always the realities of existing power structures must be recognised. But effective leaders of PHC find ways to work round the difficulties. They build strong networks of individuals and groups, as we have seen in the chapter on intersectoral collaboration, and work with them to create a 'shared vision' of how things could be different in the future. A 'shared vision' for PHC is crucial in any situation, but has to be developed within each local situation and culture. Grass-roots PHC works within the culture of specific communities, but in providing long-term and short-term support for PHC the importance of organisational culture must also be recognised. Underlying value systems and philosophies need to be taken into account, and where necessary new models have evolved. Working to overcome inertia within well established bureaucracies and institutions is a complex process requiring the skills of change agents. Similar skills are needed in grass-roots community development workers. However, the need to adopt similar approaches in 'organisational development' is not yet so widely recognised. Recognising this need and making concerted efforts to improve the skills in 'management of change' amongst those in influential positions may therefore be a critical factor in improving organisational support for PHC.

Entering the 1990s

In the field of PHC it is now reasonably clear what needs to be done in the 1990s, and this book has given some indications of what can be done. A reasonable bridgehead for PHC has been established in many countries. The need now is for consolidation of what has been achieved already and advance on a much broader front. In some ways, the early pioneering phase of PHC is over. A number of lessons have been learnt and strategies as well as techniques which are likely to be successful have been identified. What is now needed is to mobilise the forces of a wide range of institutions (for example government departments, training institutions, research bodies etc.) which have a part to play in the promotion of PHC. This implies the need for continuing reorientation within the institutions and collaborative dialogue between them. Such a process will enable most national institutions to become powerful agents of change.

To achieve this a number of activities and processes need to be generated.
1. Continuing reassessment by the Ministry of Health, other associated government departments, training institutions, district hospitals, professional associations, and non-governmental organisations of their roles and functions in relation to PHC. From such regular reviews should arise a plan of working towards achieving the goals of PHC.
2. Efforts to increase organisational capabilities for implementing change. This entails freedom in planning through decentralisation, as well as managerial skills. The need is for 'on-the-job' training and trainers who work within the organisation rather than the classroom. Currently there are a limited number of consultants who understand health priorities, management, as well as social and cultural issues. Increasingly they need to work with their counterparts. Indiscriminate change in the hope of hitting upon a workable set-up can only create confusion. Hence change in organisational arrangements, lines of command and so on must have the objective of providing effective support for the eight elements of PHC. Assessment of efficiency requires monitoring and evaluation, and the setting of specific targets as a result. Hence the managerial process

must move closer to the interface with the community. The 'training cells' being developed in Bombay and Zambia (page 72) are one way forward. Such cells bring together the skills of trainers in management with those of experienced health professionals to work systematically towards specific developments in health systems. Further experience with such cells will help to set the pattern for the 1990s.

3. A willingness to accept that health systems have often evolved in an incremental fashion as a result of crisis intervention rather than planned development. They must therefore carry defects. Constructive criticism of existing systems based on sound reasoning and accompanied by a genuine search for alternative approaches should be welcomed.

4. It is no good saying that curative oriented services must change if hospitals are still swamped with queues of patients and waiting lists. The curative trained health workers need to adapt to new roles through appropriate training programmes. There will be the need for producing relevant training curricula and texts for all levels of health workers.

5. A willingness to develop new relationships across traditional disciplines and professional lines. Many of the most innovative changes have come through 'bedfellows' from different backgrounds addressing problems in a new light, for example the Child-to-Child programme.

New issues to be addressed

After the main conceptual foundations and philosophical framework of the eighties, the coming decade is likely to focus on the 'nuts-and-bolts' aspects of PHC. In a fast-moving world a number of new issues are likely to arise. There will be new diseases and health problems demanding urgent response, for example the AIDS epidemic. There will be new man-made or natural disasters, for example famine in Africa. These challenges will test the resilience of the systems of care being established in various countries. There will clearly arise many experiences and lessons from which the more developed countries can learn as much as the developing world.

Conclusion

The drive for PHC has helped to bring health issues to the centre of the stage. As countries progress towards PHC they also build up the mechanisms for national development. A healthy population is not only the outcome but also an essential ingredient of development. Through PHC's commitment to equity, popular participation and social justice, vast numbers of people can be brought into the mainstream of the development process rather than being its passive observers. The 1990s will witness the enrichment of national life in many countries as the hitherto untapped ideas and dormant energies of vast numbers of people begin to contribute to national development. This has been witnessed already in the countries of the Pacific Basin and is likely to be repeated elsewhere.

Index